**GREAT WRITERS** CHARLES BUKOWSKI

**GREAT WRITERS**

# CHARLES BUKOWSKI

**Michael Gray Baughan**

**Foreword by Gay Brewer**

CHELSEA HOUSE
PUBLISHERS
A Haights Cross Communications Company
Philadelphia

**CHELSEA HOUSE PUBLISHERS**

VP, NEW PRODUCT DEVELOPMENT  Sally Cheney
DIRECTOR OF PRODUCTION  Kim Shinners
CREATIVE MANAGER  Takeshi Takahashi
MANUFACTURING MANAGER  Diann Grasse

**Staff for SYLVIA PLATH**

EXECUTIVE EDITOR: Matt Uhler
ASSOCIATE EDITOR: Susan Naab
EDITORIAL ASSISTANT: Sharon Slaughter
PRODUCTION EDITOR: Megan Emery
SERIES AND COVER DESIGNER: Takeshi Takahashi
COVER: © Sophie Bassouls/CORBIS SYGMA
LAYOUT: EJB Publishing Services

A Haights Cross Communications ✦ Company

http://www.chelseahouse.com

First Printing

9  8  7  6  5  4  3  2  1

Library of Congress Cataloging-in-Publication Data

Baughan, Michael Gray, 1973-
  Charles Bukowski / Michael Gray Baughan.
     p. cm. — (Great writers)
  Includes bibliographical references.
  ISBN 0-7910-7844-2
 1. Bukowski, Charles. 2. Authors, American—20th century—Biography.
3. Beat generation—Biography. I. Title. II. Great writers (Philadelphia, Pa.)
  PS3552.U4Z523 2004
  811'.54—dc22
                                              2004003393

# TABLE OF CONTENTS

IN 1993 I ACCEPTED a university job in Tennessee and immediately tested the waters there about starting a literary journal, in part to publish the work of my two favorite living poets, William Stafford and Charles Bukowski. Both men were known for their generous and democratic distribution of work to the small presses. News of the fates of poets, however, can be slow to circulate (at least in my neighborhood at the time), and only after I'd written requesting submissions did I read that Mr. Stafford had been dead for months. Mr. Bukowski, meanwhile, responded with three forceful poems, and I was delighted. I didn't yet know that he had leukemia and would also be dead before the first issue of *Poems & Plays* appeared in late spring of 1994. (A sad and ironic postscript: I learned of both deaths just in time to dedicate the inaugural issue of the journal to the poets who had inspired its inception.)

In the fourth number of *Poems & Plays* we published two additional poems by Charles Bukowski (thanks to John Martin), and, taken together, they constitute a sine qua non, an essential and indispensable example, of Bukowski's life-long concerns. "I saw the lights in the / windows, / I felt the presence of / those 3,000 people / in there. // then I turned and walked away / into the night. // and my life was touched by / magic. // and it still / is." These are the closing lines of "the 12 hour night," a narrative describing the author's parting with the post office and its numbing drudgery. Note the simultaneous empathy toward and dismissal of the lives dimming within those gray walls and wasted hours. The poem includes a trademark Bukowski paradox: his coveted isolation (isolationism?) requires the presence of the city and its crowds of disappointed/disappointing humanity—or, as our author Michael Gray Baughan states it a bit differently, "a tension between comfortable anonymity and a partially sublimated longing for recognition [that] would remain with Bukowski for the rest of his life. The missing piece of this puzzle, of course, is artistic creation, a rigorous writing life that enables, empowers, and informs, a life of gamble and magic; in short, a religious life of privacy and introspection that sustains and partially redeems everyday dreariness. "if you're going to try, / go all the way. / there is no other feeling like / that. / you will be alone with the / gods / and the nights will flame with / fire. // ... // you will ride life straight to / perfect laughter, it's / the only good fight / there is." These lines are from "roll the dice," *Poems & Plays'* companion to "the 12 hour night." Note the evangelic zeal of the narrator, the proclamation of writing's transformative power, and the invitation to come along for a hell of a ride.

A lot of bombastic and self-serving nonsense has been written about Charles Bukowski, and a lot continues to be. Years ago I quit reading the various memoirs, tell-alls, and cloudy histories by "wanna-be"s, "never-were"s, and tangential acquaintances. So, I was pleased to discover Michael Gray Baughan's new Bukowski biography for Chelsea House. Mr. Baughan stipulates that his modest but worthy aim is to provide "a useful aid and one-stop shop for anyone in search of an accessible introduction to one of America's most prolific and popular authors" (2). He accomplishes this and more, communicating the wild tale of Bukowski's life with clear-headedness, candor, style, and grace (qualities his subject greatly admired), and he's factual and detailed with a minimal amount of scholarly folderol. We get the context we need and, when some amount of interpretation is required, Baughan is consistently balanced in his assessments. He seems to get just about everything right, and I gulped down this pleasant bonbon of a biography in one sitting. I think you might find it equally tasty.

When I was reading and researching for my critical study of Bukowski's work, titled simply *Charles Bukowski* (be warned: it's loaded with end notes and analytic minutiae), I was amazed at the lack of balanced, thoughtful discussion on his massive oeuvre. On the one hand were the wild, febrile (and almost always shabbily written) rants about Bukowski's genius and deification; on the other a few, very few, cold-shouldered dismissals from the academic fortress Bukowski so energetically fingered (double entendre intentional) for a lifetime. Now, a decade after Bukowski's death, Baughan does a commendable job separating the smoke from the truth, the myth from the more complicated and interesting reality of the life, warts and all. Anyone who disagrees with much of this biography is probably somebody you're better off away from.

I do believe, though, that Mr. Baughan may be overly bleak about Charles Bukowski's present and future place in academia. Although Bukowski is still conspicuously and shamefully absent from mainstream anthologies, lots of my friends and professional colleagues read and enjoy his writing, and more than a few have come out of the closet to pepper their literature classes with a selection or two. For the reader willing to track it down and wade through some bull, more and generally better criticism seems to be appearing, and only in the whitest and deadest and most remote ivory tower does Bukowski's importance continue to be ignored. (And believe me: his massive output of writing has a lot to do with the residual snubbing. If you beginning poets have the impropriety to write and publish "too much," you too may savor the sour taste of this class distinction.) In the novel *Hollywood*, Sarah informs Henry Chinaski, Bukowski's fictional alter ego, that he's "just a natural-ass writer" (66), a deceptively simple label that explains the artist's indomitability and resistance to corruption (be it money, Hollywood, and just falling in love with one's own reviews). The writing act is essential, indeed inseparable, from the man; he just can't help it, and that's his and our good fortune. So maybe time will out; if the tower doesn't collapse by a direct assault, there's always the service entrance (and down there's where they keep the booze).

So I'm grateful for Michael Gray Baughan's nice contribution to the excavation of Bukowski's factual life from the fictions perpetuated by apostles, hangers-on, and Bukowski himself. Maybe now we can let the old man rest and get on with the lucky business of enjoying the lively, brooding, often inspired work of this "natural-ass writer." Ten years down the gritty road, new volumes of poetry and letters continue to be released, and it's good stuff. How blessed can we be?  Baughan informs us, correctly I think, that Charles Bukowski was "a man perpetually trapped between social longing and misanthropy, sovereign pride and self-loathing" (103). We discussed this earlier, and maybe you know the feeling. Around the same time that I was putting together the first issue of *Poems & Plays*, I made the acquaintance of the general editor for the long-running Twayne United States Authors Series, published at that time by Macmillan. I was interested in writing a book for the series but was hesitant to devote two years of my life to any of the subjects available: Edward Abbey, Alice Adams, Maya Angelou, Laurie Colwin, Samuel Delany, Thomas Disch, Elmore Leonard, Adrienne Rich, Susan Sontag, William Maxwell, Richard Ford, Kurt Vonnegut "revisited."  A prestigious list, no question, but also no sparks. Then, in March of 1994, I received a cryptic and enticing note: "I have just learned that the Twayne contract for a Charles Bukowski book has been cancelled. So he is up for grabs. Interested?" I liked the intrigue (never explained to me) of someone's fumbled attempt, and of course being asked to come off the bench played to my ego. By that time, though, I'd pretty much decided against contributing a volume.

The very next day after receiving the note, I was sitting in my office when the telephone rang. A friend told me that Charles Bukowski had died of cancer. I didn't know he'd been sick, and I suppose in that moment I realized I would write the book. My immediate response was to cancel classes for the day. I took a long, solitary drive in the hills, a rural landscape that I've always found meditative, spiritually necessary, and creatively rejuvenating. Bukowski, by the way, hated the country, what he considered its monotony and, yes, lack of humanity. "What are you going to do with it?" he growls during Barbet Schroeder's *The Bukowski Tapes*. And to the fledgling writer and the Bukowski "fan," that's my advice and, if I may, my warning: enjoy Baughan's fine new intro-ductory biography, but forget about trying to emulate Bukowski's life. Who in his or her right mind would want to?  Admire instead the poet's steadfast individualism and, more importantly, his darkly funny and courageous writing. There is no single, correct prescription for an artist's life, an integrated life dedicated to something dynamic, vital, and wild, one of the few lives worth living. You have to do it for yourself.

Gaylord Brewer
January 2004

GIVEN THE UNTOLD REAMS of paper and barrels of ink already devoted to the life and work of Charles Bukowski (not to mention the mountain of words carved out with his own hand), the first question any reasonable person would ask upon cracking open this latest addition is, Do we really need any more? I am not foolhardy enough to propose the definitive answer, but do feel it necessary (and possible) to justify my own small contribution.

First and foremost, I did not attempt to surpass the efforts of Neeli Cherkovski (author of *Bukowski: A Life*) or Howard Sounes (*Charles Bukowski: Locked in the Arms of a Crazy Life*). If the quality of their work made that unlikely, the more modest scope of the present work rendered it impossible. The former knew Bukowski very well during the headiest years of his career and delivered an extremely readable first-hand account, and though he included a number of factual inaccuracies, his book is filled with the kind of anecdotal detail no researcher could hope to match. The latter conducted over a hundred interviews with Bukowski's family, friends, lovers, and peers; scoured boxes of unpublished letters, official documents, and other materials; and unearthed many never before seen photos. The resulting work is by far the most thoroughly researched book on Bukowski ever written, and will in all likelihood remain the definitive biography. I owe a huge debt to both of these authors and have made every effort to give them credit for any information I have drawn solely from them. About midway through completion of this project, I also became aware of Aubrey Malone's *The Hunchback of East Hollywood: A Biography of Charles Bukowski* (2003). While I, personally, did not draw any specific information from this book, Malone's emphasis on how Bukowski's life impacted his work and vice versa may prove helpful to those who feel such analysis is lacking elsewhere.

In writing my own book on Bukowski, I tried to steer a middle course between these examples by delivering an engaging introduction to Bukowski's life without sacrificing any accuracy or scholarship. Where relevant, I have highlighted the discrepancies between existing accounts of given events or perceptions, and pointed to possible means of rectifying them. I also draw extensively from Bukowski's own correspondence to further explore the hidden side of the man and, wherever possible, allow him to speak for himself. Furthermore, I cite many other works (some of which were still unpublished when Cherkovski and Sounes wrote their books) that will prove helpful to any student wishing to conduct additional research. Of particular value in tracking Bukowski's varied publishing history was Aaron Krumhansl's *A Descriptive Bibliography of the Primary Publications of Charles Bukowski.* Gay Brewer's book, *Charles Bukowski,* also proved indispensable with its cogent analysis of the author's mammoth oeuvre and comprehensive (and annotated) bibliography.

Most of all I endeavored to rescue Bukowski from the one-dimensional prison to which he has been confined all too often by cult fans and snide academics alike. The myth of Bukowski as the wildman laureate of skid row (and nothing more or less) has robbed him of both his essential humanity (the right to be mutable, complex, even hypocritical) and a well-earned place in the canon of twentieth-century literature. In sketching a more subtly shaded portrait I have not shied away from subjective assessments when I felt a point needed emphasis, but neither have I left any such judgments unchallenged, if contradictory evidence exists. If nothing else, I hope this book provides a useful research aid and one-stop shop for anyone in search of an accessible introduction to one of America's most prolific and popular authors.

# CHAPTER ONE

# Portrait of the Artist
# as a Young Outcast

*The first thing I remember is being under some-thing. It was a table, I saw a table leg, I saw the legs of the people, and a portion of the tablecloth hanging down. It was dark under there. I liked being under there....*

—Charles Bukowski, *Ham on Rye*

HE WAS A MAN of many names. Born and baptized Heinrich Karl, later Americanized to Henry Charles, known as Hank to his friends and lovers, "Buk" to his early admirers and collaborators in the small press, the pseudonymous Henry Chinaski to his legion of readers, and the "Dirty Old Man of American Letters" to both fans and detractors, who relish and decry his gritty, gutter-mouthed candor with equal zeal. Though used interchangeably in the pages that follow, each of these names carries a slightly dif-ferent connotation, each identifies distinct personality traits and legacies, and each is a combination of hardcore reality and (some-times self-) perpetuated myth. The real man lies somewhere between these names. In some ways, particularly in regard to the treatment he has received from academia, he is still hiding under the table that he described at the beginning of *Ham on Rye*, a fic-tionalized recounting of his childhood years:

I felt good under the table. Nobody seemed to know that I was there. There was sunlight upon the rug and on the legs of the people. I liked the sunlight. The legs of the people were not interesting, not like the tablecloth which hung down, not like the table leg, not like the sunlight.

(*Ham on Rye*, 9)

This tension between comfortable anonymity and a partially sublimated longing for recognition ("sunlight") would remain with Bukowski for the rest of his life. As would the misanthropy, the solipsism, and the desire to express things simply, in a way that everyone could understand. In the paragraph following the one quoted above, Bukowski symbolically touches upon other major themes that run through his life and career:

"Then there is nothing ... then a Christmas tree. Candles. Bird ornaments; birds with small berry branches in the beaks. A star. Two large people fighting, screaming. People eating, always people eating. I ate too. My spoon was bent so that if I wanted to eat I had to pick the spoon up with my right hand. If I picked it up with my left hand, the spoon bent away from my mouth. I wanted to pick the spoon up with my left hand."

(*Ham on Rye*, 9)

Hot-blooded conflict; overindulgence as a balm for the pain of living; a system stacked against him—all are ideas that Bukowski returns to again and again in his writings, in a constant fight to exorcise his early traumas and all the ones that followed. It was a fight he never won, but his readers get a ringside seat and those who can stand the squalor of his settings and the frankness of his speech are rewarded with a degree of truth and realism too often lacking in literature, as well as a hard-won grace and humor that just might help them through their darkest days.

In *Ham on Rye*, Bukowski gives his under-the-table reverie a date of 1922. If that is correct, the setting would have been the same apartment in the wedge-shaped building at the corner of Aktienstrasse, in Andernach, Germany, where he was born August

16, 1920. His father, Henry senior, was an American G.I. stationed in Andernach after the war as part the U.S. army of occupation. His mother, Katharina Fett, was a German seamstress whose brother, Heinrich, ran a canteen for the American troops; it was there that Heinrich met the tall, curly haired sergeant who would marry his sister. The two men became fast friends, especially after Henry began bringing meat and other hard-to-come-by items to a Fett household suffering from postwar deprivations. Henry also spoke their language, a product of his own German ancestry. His father, Leonard had left the fatherland in the 1880s and met Emilie Krause, another German émigré, in Cleveland. The pair fell in love, married, and moved to Pasadena, California, where Henry and his three brothers and two sisters were born.

Katharina played hard to get at first, but Henry's persistence and cultural familiarity eventually softened her guard and the two became lovers. Soon thereafter, Katharina found herself pregnant. Bukowski often claimed he was born out of wedlock, but according to Howard Sounes, author of *Charles Bukowksi: Locked in the Arms of a Crazy Life*, Andernach city records indicate Henry and Katharina were married on July 15, 1920, a month before little Heinrich came along. At the time, Henry was working as a building contractor, but times were tough in postwar Germany, and before long they moved to nearby Coblenz in search of more work. Less than a year after that, Henry decided to return to the U.S. with his family in the hopes of finding a better life.

Back in the States, Henry quickly Americanized his foreign-born wife and child, changing their names to Kate and Henry, Jr. They landed in Baltimore just long enough for Henry senior to work up the money to travel west, back to California.

The Bukowskis were a quarrelsome clan, headed up by hard-drinking Leonard, a veteran of the Kaiser's army who did reasonably well in America as a carpenter and general contractor in the construction boom that birthed Los Angeles. His wife Emilie was a strict Baptist who left her alcoholic husband sometime around 1920 to live in another of the houses he owned in Pasadena, but not without taking a good bit of Leonard's money with her. Bukowski had vivid memories of this "small house under an overhanging mass of pepper trees" and the hearty meals his grandmother cooked up and presided over with boastful claims that she would outlive them all (*Ham on Rye,* 10). He also remembers the canaries she kept, the cages covered each night with white hoods, and the piano he plinked away at while the grownups talked. The random notes annoyed his father, who yelled at the boy to stop, but Grandma Emilie always came to his defense.

Henry Bukowski settled his family into a small place on Trinity Street, near downtown Los Angeles. He and his wife had aspirations of upward mobility, but in the meantime Henry settled for a milkman job at the L.A. Creamery. Within three years they moved again, to a bungalow on Virginia Road. On weekends they occasionally took their Model T out to picnic in the orange groves or visit Santa Monica Beach, but even in these pleasant surroundings, life around Bukowski's father was always full of tension and the threat of sudden rages over minor mistakes. By all accounts, Henry senior was a thoroughly bitter man who constantly bad-mouthed his siblings for minor faults and eschewed his father entirely. Bukowski only remembers one or two dramatic visits with his grandfather Leonard, during which his parents sat in the car and refused to come into the house, their only explanation that the old man drank and had "bad breath." Likely exhibiting a bit of empathetic projection, Bukowski's memory of his dipsomaniac paternal grandfather comes off as a bit whitewashed—the kind but misunderstood old man who, during their brief but emotionally weighty encounters, gave his grandson a gold watch and the Iron Cross he earned in Germany.

When Bukowski began attending Virginia Road Grammar School, his parents often sent him to school dressed in precious little outfits and forbade him from playing with other children, lest he dirty his clothes. They tried to cultivate an air of superiority and were deathly afraid of giving off the merest hint of impropriety. The situation only worsened when it became evident that young Henry suffered from dyslexia and the other children began to tease him about his sissy clothes, his lingering accent, and an *uber*-Kraut forename that they tauntingly shortened to "Heinie." As a result, Bukowski was quickly alienated from his peers and developed a self-defensive surliness that became one of his main personality traits. Soon enough, the inevitable happened: Bukowski got into a fight. He claimed a bully threw the first punch, but the other boys blamed it on him. Whatever the case, Bukowski ended up in the principal's office and recalls a protracted battle of wills with an administrator hell-bent on belittling and frightening the boy by continually constricting an iron-grip handshake until Bukowksi cried for mercy. But the punishment did not end there. Forced to deliver a note to his parents, young Henry suffered woeful condemnations from his mother and his first real beating from his father. Both seemed more concerned about the shame his actions would bring to them than the situation at school that caused the altercation. Bukowski took the beating and said nothing. Not yet ten years old and his skin was already beginning to thicken.

Sometime during his grammar school years, the family moved again, to a bigger house at 2122 Longwood Avenue. There Bukowski was given a slightly longer leash and allowed to make friends with some of the neighborhood kids, who dubbed him "Hank." Bukowski liked the nickname and it stuck but, having seldom joined in before, he was far behind the other kids in coordination and athletic ability. Many embarrassing moments ensued at school and on local playgrounds where Hank's inadequacies were put on full display. In his writings and interviews, Bukowski often gives conflicting portrayals of his rank in the playground hierarchy during his adolescent years. He alternately claims he was both a loner and a leader of a pack of misfits, a perpetual victim and a fearless tough guy, a gawky misfit and a heroic late-bloomer. The reality was probably more jejune; outside his own mind Hank was likely a marginal character that inspired neither love nor hate. If his peers felt anything towards him, it was probably pity.

One day Henry asked his son to mow the lawn and handed down precise instructions for how to do so. In what would become an oft-repeated episode in Bukowski's childhood lore (bolstered by its inclusion in *Ham on Rye*), his father insisted that "not one hair" stand higher than the rest. As anyone who has ever cut a lawn can corroborate, such exacting standards are nearly impos-

/eitmotif

sible to meet. Every time Henry Bukowski made an inspection he found an errant blade, and he beat the boy for these unforgivable transgressions. Katherine did nothing to stop the beatings and even participated in the ludicrous judging process. She too had long been victim of her husband's physical and emotional abuse and preferred silent solidarity to anything that might provoke him. As a result, Hank lost whatever remaining shred of respect he had for his parents and began to think of them as callous strangers and more irrefutable evidence of a society aligned against him.

Another pivotal event from grammar school resulted from his fifth-grade teacher's suggestion that the students attend President Hoover's visit to the L.A. Coliseum and write an essay about the experience. Hank's detailed and dramatic submission was singled out for special praise and read to the class as an example of great writing. The insecure boy was greatly surprised and pleased by this rare show of positive reinforcement, especially because he had never attended the presidential address and had fabricated the entire essay. Involuntarily admitting this fact to the teacher after class only seemed to increase his achievement in her eyes. The experience had a confusing effect on Hank. On the one hand he was encouraged to write more, as a means of getting attention and relieving his social alienation. On the other, he became even more convinced that "people were fools," who only wanted to be told "beautiful lies." (*Ham on Rye*, 84). Consequently, he also lost a measure of respect for the very people who could provide his salvation—his readers. In the years to come this love-hate reaction to the attention his writing earned him became a Bukowski leitmotif, driving him to disrespect and alienate just about everyone who got too close.

The onset of puberty and the Depression only exacerbated an already bad situation. Henry lost his milkman job, forcing Katherine to earn what little she could by cleaning the houses of wealthier families. Despite this added tension, Hank managed to end his father's regular beatings by maintaining an eerie silence that eventually unnerved his old man. These private torments, however, were replaced by the very public onslaught of *acne vulgaris* so acute that Hank missed a semester of his first year in high school while undergoing months of painful treatments at the Los Angeles County Hospital, where doctors rudely marveled at the size of the boils while lancing them with an electric needle. They tried other methods—ultraviolet rays and salve-soaked bandages—but nothing seemed to help and eventually the free treatments were halted when the hospital discovered his father had found a job at the Los Angeles County Museum. Mortified by his appearance, Hank completely withdrew from society, refusing to see even the few friends who stopped by to check on him. It was during this time that he wrote his first short story, a far-fetched fantasy based on the exploits of Baron Manfred Von Richthofen, the legendary World War I pilot otherwise known as the Red Baron. The plot was outlandish and improbable, but once again Hank turned to real life people and events as his primary sources.

Several years before, Hank had begun to take refuge in public libraries, relishing the time alone but often struggling to find literature to which he could relate. During his time away from school, isolated by his affliction, Hank began to read with renewed fervor, diving headlong into Sinclair Lewis, D.H. Lawrence, and the early stories of Hemingway. The last of these would prove a lifelong influence, inspiring Hank to write simply and honestly, without embellishment. He gravitated towards works that reciprocated his outsider misanthropy and those which depicted a harsh, cruel world that mirrored his own. *Catcher in the Rye* is a perfect example, and although Bukowski was born too early to read it in his adolescence, it became an instant favorite when he did.

Bukowski claims that he and his father argued over which high school he was going to attend. The story goes that Hank preferred nearby Polytechnic High, but his father still had high hopes for his only son and enrolled the boy against his wishes in the better-reputed Los Angeles High. Bukowski also claims L.A. High was a school for rich kids and snobs, but his contemporaries maintain it was a public school like any other, with students from all levels of society, and that Bukowski went there simply because it was closest to his house. Regardless, Hank clearly felt ostracized. Despite efforts to eat more healthily, his acne spread to his chest and back, so he joined ROTC to avoid having to change in front of the other kids for gym class. But the military training had its own gruesome drawbacks—often he would rupture one or more of his boils while drilling with his rifle and the blood and puss would soil his uniform.

Things weren't any better at home. His mother lost her job cleaning houses, exacerbating their financial woes. Before he was finally able to find work at the museum, Henry Bukowski had become so embarrassed by his unemployment that he began driving off in his car each morning to make the neighbors think he was working. Then, during the interview for the museum job, he lied about having a college degree. Hank was all too aware of these deceptions and they did nothing to divest him of the notion that his father was a hypocrite and a slave to the status quo. Hank began to sneak out of his bedroom window after his parents turned in and visit bars downtown, where apparently the bouncers mistook his acne scars for signs of maturity. He met a few older boys—lowlifes and petty criminals, mostly, and even one married man who plied them with whiskey and provided a spare apartment where they often held drinking contests. Despite his inexperience, Bukowski outlasted the other boys, foreshadowing the decades of heavy drinking to come. They also attended burlesque shows, giving Hank his first taste of women. No doubt this exposure at such a young age to the seedy side of sexuality and social drinking played a large role in establishing Hank's future relationship patterns, in which sex and alcohol played the primary catalysts. It also dictated the type of women to whom he would be attracted—beautiful but damaged *femme fatales* whose craving for attention played havoc with Hank's insecurities and provoked a manic jealousy he was powerless to control. But all that would come later. At the time, Hank was just a pimply teen who felt certain no woman could ever find him attractive. So he drank and he rebelled.

On the whole he managed to escape his parent's detection, but eventually he always slipped up. On one night in particular he arrived home too drunk to try the window and went around to the front door and knocked. His mother woke up first, saw the state he was in and woke her husband, who refused to unlock the door.

When Hank tried ramming it with his shoulder his father, fearing a public scene, finally let him in, but the exertion and the alcohol got the best of Hank and he threw up on the living room rug. Enraged, his father grabbed him by the neck and tried to push his face into the vomit, saying that is what you did when "a dog shits on the rug." Hank begged him to stop but his father kept pushing. A rage welled up inside of the boy, and when he finally broke free, he punched his father in the face. When Henry crumpled to the floor his wife panicked and began to rake her son's face with her fingernails. Fortunately, the row eventually subsided without anyone getting seriously hurt, and even had a positive outcome: his father never laid a hand on Hank again.

High school ended the way it began for Bukowski, with him on the outside—literally. In a scene worthy of Hollywood, Hank spent his senior prom alone, gazing at his peers through the gymnasium windows, overlaying the vision of their easy grace and smiling faces with the ugliness of his own reflection in the glass. For a moment he was able to convince himself his time of happiness would come. "Someday my dance would begin." (*Ham on Rye*, 194). Then a janitor appeared, shining a flashlight in his face and demanding that Bukowski leave, despite the latter's claims that he actually belonged there.

Graduation proved equally traumatic. Bukowski's lack of prospects caused another fight with his parents, who disparaged the boy and predicted failure and poverty for him. All he wanted was to get out on his own. He hoped his writing would show the way.

Unsure of what else to do, Hank took a stock boy job at a Sears Roebuck, schlepping merchandise to the various departments. It was a lousy fit from the start. His boss chided him for the smallest infractions and lorded his power over Hank's livelihood with despotic arrogance. His fellow employees were all lifers—sad cases who long ago had given up the dream of anything better or else petty midlevel clerks who enjoyed stepping on the fingers of anyone trying to climb the ladder after them. Bukowski certainly didn't help himself by being sarcastic and bitter, perpetually walking around with a chip on his shoulder bigger than his oversized head. In a pattern that repeated itself over and over again for more than a decade, Bukowksi kept the job for a week or so, did something to get himself fired, and then moved on.

In the fall of 1939, Bukowksi starting taking Journalism and English courses at Los Angeles City College, with the help of a government scholarship. He didn't have an academic plan, really, just thought working at a newspaper might be more interesting than punching a time clock. The war in Europe had begun and, in typical Bukowski fashion, he played devil's advocate by publicly supporting Hitler and Nazism. His parents had long been associated with the Deutsche Haus, a local meeting place for German-Americans located not too far from their home, and his mother had often praised Hitler as a hero to the working class. The Deutsche Haus had a small bookstore attached to it that featured many German works translated into in English, and it was there that Bukowski apparently discovered *Mein Kampf.* He must have experienced a powerful attraction to this fellow outcast and misanthrope, whose own father had also tried to dictate his future and was constantly full of criticism. The extent of Bukowski's political involvement, however, was limited to attending a few meetings of the German-American Bund and sending a couple outspoken letters to local newspapers. In later years, he characterized his Nazi sympathies as merely a continuation of his anti-conformist streak, coupled with a desire to shock the status quo; but like everything else that came out of his mouth or his typewriter, these rationalizations should be taken with a grain of salt.

Thankfully, there were more powerful influences on Bukowski's psychological development than Hitler. Chief among them was novelist John Fante, whose spare prose and underdog protagonists served as lifelong models for Bukowski's own writings. *Ask the Dusk* was a particular favorite and remained one of the few works that Bukowski continued to praise long after he lost faith in the latter-day works of better-known writers like Hemingway and Henry Miller. Hank empathized strongly with the book's hero, Arturo Bandini, a fellow aspiring writer and the child of immigrant parents who ends up in a seedy part of Los Angeles called Bunker Hill in search of life lessons and love. Bukowski was thrilled by the way Fante brought the familiar neighborhood to life and inspired by Fante's ability to find powerful subject matter in such a quotidian reality.

Despite this growing love for literature, Bukowski continued to be an indifferent student at City College. School authorities put him on academic probation and threatened to take away his scholarship. There were exceptions, when words and ideas flowed out of him spontaneously, almost involuntarily. He remembered one writing class in which he was assigned one piece per week; by the end of the term he had easily surpassed the quota, submitting dozens more than any other student. The professor kept a running tally of his prolific output and, as with his grammar school essay on Hoover's visit, the encouraging feedback Bukowski received as a result became a key step forward in the development of his self-image as a writer. On the whole, however, he disliked his professors, whom he considered leftist egotistical bores. He became friends with a few classmates, among them fellow writer Robert Stanton Baume, whose short fiction Hank enjoyed, and Robert and Beverly Knox, who contradict the monolithic image of wild man Bukowski by describing him during these formative years as shy and civil. Hank dreamed of becoming a professional writer but lacked any clear idea of how to make that dream a reality.

Bukowski's college enrollment temporarily placated his parents. His father still had major doubts about his son's ability to hold down a job or become a productive member of society, but he reasoned that earning a degree was a step in the right direction and seemed at least willing to continue providing for Hank so long as his son stayed the course and showed some ambition. The Bukowskis even bought their son a typewriter to help with his coursework. That brief period of support came to a dramatic end one day when Hank ran into his mother on his way home from class. Katherine was in quite a state. Apparently, his father had discovered a cache of stories in a drawer in Hank's bedroom and become so enraged by the thought of his son wasting time better spent on his studies that he heaved the typewriter onto their front lawn, together with the manuscripts and a pile of Hank's clothes. Katherine warned her son that his father threatened to kill him when he got home. Instead of being scared, Hank was incensed by the news and rushed home for the inevitable showdown. Seeing his things strewn helter-skelter across the lawn he so hated to trim only angered him all the more, and Bukowski called for his father to come out and fight him like a man. When his father never materialized, Hank collected his things, borrowed a little money from his mother, and found a cheap room downtown on Temple Street.

Finally free of his parents, Hank discovered other ways of getting in trouble. A visit from Robert Baume, who had since left school to join the marines, turned violent when Hank began to disparage the man's literary heroes and patriotic choice of vocation. The freewheeling fight only ended when the marine knocked Bukowski out cold, and Hank awoke the next morning to find his alarmed landlady calling to him from behind the door. Hank ignored her entreaties and she finally went away, but when he next emerged from his room he found a handyman on apparent sentry duty pretending to pound nails into the carpet. Paranoid he had been set up for some kind of ambush, Bukowski packed what little he had and grabbed his typewriter, but when he tried to leave the handyman got in his way and asked him where he thought he was going. Cornered, Hank bashed the man's head with the portable typewriter and took off running. The only place he could think to go was Bunker Hill, the sketchy neighborhood John Fante had immortalized in *Ask the Dust* and a haven for people trying not to be found. Bukowski rented a room there and tried to plot his next move. He could not have known it at the time, but his life among the drunks, the hookers, and the dispossessed had only just begun.

# CHAPTER TWO

# First and Last Words

*I looked at my father, at his hands, his face, his eye-brows, and I knew that this man had nothing to do with me. He was a stranger. My mother was non-existent. I was cursed. Looking at my father I saw nothing but indecent dullness....*

—Charles Bukowski, *Ham on Rye*

BUKOWSKI DROPPED OUT of City College not long after leaving home and settled deeper into his outcast existence, writing stories of alienation in his dingy Bunker Hill digs. For the next six months he eked out a living at a couple dead-end jobs like cleaning the sides of boxcars with other young roustabouts at the Southern Pacific railroad yards. Another encounter with college pal Robert Baume ended with the pair barhopping downtown until a news bulletin broke over a transistor radio and informed them the Japanese had just bombed Pearl Harbor. Baume again tried to convince Hank to enlist, but Hank simply could not relate to his friend's bravado and nationalism. To his way of thinking, military duty demanded a mindless enslavement. After accompanying Baume to the bus station, Bukowski said goodbye to his friend for the last time; Baume was later killed in the Pacific during his tour.

Pressure to enlist also came from his father, during those times when Hank returned home to borrow money or bum a meal, and the situation only worsened when Germany declared war on the U.S. Fed up, Hank decided he had to get out of L.A.

He saved some money from his job at the train yards and caught a bus to New Orleans in early 1942, with the idea of gaining some real-world experience to ground his writing. En route he met a pretty redhead named Dulcey Ditmore who showed enough interest in him to suggest he stop off awhile in her hometown of Fort Worth. Bukowski declined at first and they parted ways, but fellow passengers on the bus laid into him for throwing away a chance at love and Hank eventually acquiesced, getting off in Dallas, backtracking through Texas, and ultimately finding Dulcey with the help of a story-hungry newspaper columnist. The reunion turned sour, though, when Dulcey revealed she was engaged to a guy in the navy and began proselytizing Hank with talk about the helping hand of God. Hank split town almost immediately, but his desperate need for companionship is evidenced by the fact that he continued to write Dulcey for some time thereafter.

In New Orleans Hank found cheap housing and a job at a magazine distributor, packing and verifying orders. The work was dull and the pay meager and once again he lasted just long enough to make some money for rent. With the exception of one other short stint setting type at a local newspaper, Hank spent the rest of his time in New Orleans writing in his room and occasionally submitting stories to magazines in New York. All were rejected but sometimes the responses contained a few words of encouragement that helped sustain him. In "young in New Orleans," he wrote:

being lost,
being crazy maybe
is not so bad
if you can be
that way:
undisturbed.

New Orleans gave me
that.
nobody ever called
my name.

Evidently that life of simple anonymity was not enough to keep him in the Big Easy, though, because Bukowski made plans a few months later to head back to California by joining a railroad crew bound for Sacramento. Hank encountered little camaraderie among his fellow workers but he did find a friend in the nameless narrator of Dostoyevsky's *Notes from the Underground*, which he happened upon in an El Paso public library and promptly read in one sitting.

Another favorite piece of literature that Bukowski first read during this period was Knut Hamsun's *Hunger*. Both works champion the individual's right to chart his own course, irrespective of social norms or expectations, and both provided models of writing as the ultimate act of sovereignty. Bolstered by such examples, and a confidence born of his self-sustainment, however tenuous, Bukowski could return to California not as a failed wanderer but as a man who had reaffirmed his prime directive.

Out of money, hungry, and probably in desperate need of some quiet time in one place, Hank returned to his parents' house on Longwood Avenue. His mother apparently welcomed him back but his father threatened to charge him rent and Hank continued to provoke him with drunken, late-night disturbances. Another short-lived job at an auto parts warehouse earned Hank enough to move to San Francisco in the spring of 1942, where he found much more tolerable work driving for the Red Cross. The Bay Area also afforded him a nice place to live, in a rooming house with a view of the Golden Gate Bridge and a charitable landlady who kept cold beers on hand for him and offered him unlimited use of her gramophone to play the classical records he swapped at a second hand store. All in all it was the sweetest set up he had found yet, but good or bad, Hank could not seem to get it together—he blew it by showing up late to work one day. Unemployed again, he fell back into his standard routine: drinking, writing, drinking, submitting stories, and more drinking.

Hank left San Francisco later that year and spent the next three years bouncing around the country in a never-ending string of odd jobs, boarding houses, drunken benders, and brief but shamefaced respites at his parents' house. In a St. Louis basement he stuffed boxes full of ladies dresses. In New York he took another stock boy job and shivered in his West Coast clothes. In Philadelphia he worked as a shipping clerk for Fairmount Motor Products and, when that gig ended, survived by gophering for fellow lushes in a downtown bar, placing their bets with bookies, making lunchtime runs to the deli, and perpetually picking fights with a hulking bar-back named Frank McGilligan. Inevitably Bukowski took a beating but his indomitable spunk always earned him a few drinks and the respect of the bar. Nearly a half-century later, this last locale would serve as the setting for *Barfly*, the film Barbet Schroeder directed from a script by Bukowski (see Chapter Seven).

Three pivotal events occurred during these lost years that would shape Bukowski's future in myriad ways: losing his virginity, publishing his first story, and getting imprisoned for draft dodging. The first was important not so much because it was memorable or sensual but because it lifted Hank over the hump (so to speak) of his unchecked insecurity and augured the onset of a late-blooming virility potent enough to transform him from ugly duckling to veritable womanizer. By all accounts the lucky lady was a fat girl in Philadelphia who was just intrigued enough by his inebriated entreaties to let him have his way. Despite her girth and homely looks, Bukowski was still so convinced of his own repulsiveness that he offered her money the following morning. Whether she was in fact a prostitute remains somewhat unclear, though she quickly became one in the stories he told of the experience.

Despite a growing collection of rejection slips, Hank set his sights high and doggedly continued to submit his stories to some of the most prestigious magazines in the country, like *The Atlantic Monthly* and *Story*. An editor at the latter publication named Whit Burnett, who had a penchant for discovering unpublished writers (most notably William Saroyan), often wrote longer than typical responses, occasionally with constructive criticism, so Bukowski just kept submitting to him until Burnett finally accepted a witty little autobiographical piece titled "Aftermath of a Lengthy Rejection Slip." He chose "Charles Bukowski" as his byline because it had a more literary ring to it than Henry. He also felt compelled to expunge any connection to his father. Like most struggling writers, Bukowski was elated beyond all proportion by his first publication and was soon envisioning a major breakthrough. He even moved to New York in the spring of 1944 in the hopes of launching his literary career, but when the issue of *Story* came out he discovered, to his great disappointment and embarrassment, that "Aftermath" had been presented among the end pages of the magazine. Convinced it had only been accepted as a lark, to dam his flood of submissions, Hank never sent anything to *Story* or corresponded with Whit Burnett again.

The compositional slight accompanying his first publication was nothing compared to the trouble that found Bukowski when the law came looking. The story behind Bukowski's draft record and eventual arrest is another one of those situations in the author's life when fact and fiction bleed across their borders. At least two versions exist, no doubt resulting from a combination of Hank's alcohol-addled memory and his tendency to edit unflattering personal details. Hank's first biographer and close friend, Neeli Cherkovski, wrote (while Bukowski was still alive) that his subject avoided conscription by drawing an unusually high draft number. More recently, Howard Sounes cited the reason as a failed psychiatric test and the resulting diagnosis of "4-F" or "unfit for military service." Whatever the case, Bukowski never technically dodged the draft. He merely failed to keep the authorities properly appraised of his whereabouts. Nevertheless, on July 22, 1944 (Sounes cites new sources to peg the date two years later than Cherkovski, 255), two FBI agents showed up at Hank's room in Philadelphia and arrested him on suspicion of draft dodging.

Bukowski was sent to Moyamensing Prison, a gothic detention center in Philadelphia for debtors and men awaiting trial that had once held Edgar Allan Poe. Because it was low-security and housed no violent criminals, he had a relatively easy time behind bars. He won so much money shooting craps that he was able to arrange quality food deliveries to his cell, which he initially shared with a notorious con man named Courtney Taylor. After complaining about the teeming bed bugs, Hank was later paired with another inmate who apparently went by the name of Tara Bubba. His cell-mate was later depicted memorably in the short story "Doing Time With Public Enemy No. 1" as the madman who succinctly summarized prison life by saying nothing all day but "Tara Bubba eat, Tara Bubba sheet."

Bukowski was released 17 days later, after the allegations of drafting dodging were cleared up, but he was forced to re-register and take another battery of tests. The results of his second psychological examination also remain ambiguous. Sounes says he "failed" it, while Cherkovski and Bukowski himself describe a sympathetic shrink who recognized Hank's artistic temperament and saved him from the brutality of war. Regardless of these minor inconsistencies, the outcomes were the same: a second reprieve from military duty, an increased disconnect with society at large, and a couple of great stories to tell.

Oddly enough, Bukowski responded to these significant life events by putting a virtual moratorium on his writing for nearly ten years and sinking even further into alcoholism and depression. Perhaps to help explain why his career stalled after his initial success, Bukowski often claimed he stopped writing entirely during this time, but that isn't true. As Sounes has shown, there is proof to the contrary, albeit spotty, in his publishing record. In the spring of 1946, Caresse and Harry Crosby, founders of Black Sun Press and *Portfolio* magazine, published his story "20 Tanks from Kasseldown" alongside works by Jean Genet, Federico Garcia Lorca, Henry Miller and Jean-Paul Sartre. In a pitiful and ironic twist, given Hank's deliberate choice of byline, his father took a copy of *Portfolio* to his job at the LA Country Museum one day and passed off the work as his own, instinctively zeroing in on one of the few things that could have actually increased his son's disgust for him.

Sounes also identifies this period as when Bukowski first began to write poetry, the mode in which his fame was ultimately secured, although Bukowski himself claimed the shift occurred much later. In 1946, four of his early poems and two short stories ("The Reason Behind Reason" and "Love, Love, Love") appeared in consecutive issues of *Matrix*, a low-budget publication out of Philadelphia. Presaging the style and content of his many works to come, the poems were gritty and laconic, the stories autobiographical sketches of a man named Chelaski, just a few letters different from his later pseudonym, Henry Chinaski.

Bukowski's semi-hiatus is fairly easily explained when one combines his worsening alcoholism with the intensity of his relationship with Jane Cooney Baker, the fallout from which would conversely catalyze one of Bukowski's most productive periods.

They met in the Glenview Bar, one of Hank's main haunts after he returned to Los Angeles for good in late 1946. Hank got a room downtown, within walking distance of the bar, and one night he spied an older blond sitting solo and looking melancholy. Hank was immediately attracted to her tragic bearing and slightly faded good looks. That his come-ons were met with a hard-edged indifference and a weary fatalism only increased his interest, and it did not hurt that she was every bit the boozer he was and willing to sleep with him the night they met.

Ten years his senior, Jane was already well on her way to alcoholic oblivion by the time she met Charles Bukowski. Traumatized by the early demise of her father, impregnated and married just out of high school (in that order), widowed by the drunk-driving death of a man who may or may not have divorced her just before he died, and too drunk and despondent to care for her two children, Jane Baker put to shame any claims Bukowski made to having lived a hard life. Given her background, it was no wonder, really, that she drank to forget her troubles, that she had a violent streak, and that her antics often edged close to outright dementia. Nor it is any great mystery what drew them together. Any woman offering him companionship would have grabbed Bukowski's attention—but Jane matched his hatred for the rest of the world, could stand her own (emotionally and physically) whenever they fought, and, if anything, drank even more than he did. The only real unknown in the equation is how they managed to survive together for so many years without killing one another or stumbling into some senseless misfortune. That the cops were occasionally called in to intercede probably helped them on that score. Bukowski's FBI file reports at least three arrests for drunkeness, in 1948, '49, and '51.

Hank and Jane shacked up together in a series of apartments downtown, on at least one occasion posing as a married couple to secure a lease. By all accounts their relationship had a surfeit of passion, swinging wildly from heated arguments to equally incendiary lovemaking. Most of their fights apparently stemmed from Hank's jealous rages over Jane's tendency to flirt with whoever was willing to pay her bar tab. If Hank was employed at the time, he could fill that role and keep her company, at least during his off hours, but more often than not being Jane's constant drinking buddy led to losing whatever jobs he could get and the vicious cycle started all over again. It would be over-reaching, though, to characterize all their time together as contentious and debased. Even a cursory review of the poems and stories that Bukowski wrote about his time with Jane contain as many instances of humor, hard-won grace, and underdog solidarity as they do squalor and indignity. Jane even worked for a time to help ends meet, and Bukowski would lovingly prepare a bath for her when she got home. Nonetheless, few would dispute that Hank's first relationship established a destructive pattern that doomed nearly all those that followed.

In early 1952, Bukowski finally found a stable source of income, in the unlikeliest of places: the post office. A two-week temp assignment helping out with the Christmas excess in 1950 led to him being hired full-time a year and a half later, and Hank stuck with the job for the next three. The irony of becoming a cog in one of the largest bureaucratic machines of all was not lost on Hank, but he found the work soft, at least until he had to interact with his coworkers. In any case, something about the mail suited him because future stints working for the United States Postal Service would run even longer and ultimately produce *Post Office*, his first novel.

Hank's many years of self-abuse caught up with him in the spring of 1955. Feeling ill one day at the post office, he decided to go home and sleep it off, but when he woke in the morning he was vomiting blood. Lacking insurance or savings, he was taken to the charity ward of Los Angeles County Hospital and spent a terrible night in a room full of equally forsaken men before an X-ray was taken. The news was not good. Bukowski had a bleeding ulcer and without a blood transfusion would likely die. A nurse even suggested he call in a priest. The problem was, he only qualified for a transfusion if he could prove he or someone in his family had donated. Bukowski's father was the only one who could make such a claim and, in this way, Bukowski became indebted for his life a second time to the man he hated most. In some families, and most literature, the resultant scene in the hospital would have played out like a hymn to redemption and forgiveness, with father and son burying the hatchet and forging a new bond. But the animosity between them ran too deep, and there would be no reconciliation with his father, then or thereafter. The way Bukowski remembered it, they nearly came to blows in his recovery room.

He was released from the hospital with the admonition that he would die if he ever drank again. Greatly weakened and once again chafing under the yolk of an anal, unsympathetic supervisor, Bukowski resigned from his job at the post office and began to write with increased prolificacy. Poems began pouring out of him at a rapid clip. He did not, however, stop drinking. Even if he had wanted to, living with Jane would have made that impossible. Tentative sessions brought on no more physical breakdowns and so he dove back into the bottle as if nothing had ever happened.

Losing his post office pay meant Bukowski had to find another source of income. Apparently it was Jane who suggested the horse-track. Bukowski barely knew of its existence, let alone how to bet, but nevertheless one day they set out for Hollywood Park and within a few hours Bukowski was already devising a system. Characteristically, it was based on betting against the majority. Uncharacteristically, luck was on his side, and they had three winners in the first day alone, one of which brought home fifty dollars. Bukowski was hooked. He had no taste for the chaotic atmosphere, but the possibility of earning money by guts and ingenuity alone, outside the workaday world of bosses and offices, seemed almost too good to be true. They served liquor at the track, and that, combined with the thrill of the races and his continued winning streak, all but sealed his fate as an inveterate horse gambler.

His relationship with Jane took a downswing when she began to accuse him of cheating on her and then her daughter arrived out of nowhere, pregnant and in need of care and a place to stay. Hank and Jane's relationship had been rocky all along, with periodic cooling-off periods and heated reunions, but this time the separation was lasting. Hank moved out and spent his additional free time writing poetry, gradually refining his straight-shooting style and keeping to his earthy subject matter. Distrustful of the major periodicals, he began to look for publication opportunities in the little magazines and journals. One day he saw an advertisement calling for submissions to *Harlequin* magazine, published out of Wheeler, Texas. Bukowski sent a sheaf of poems on a whim, never expecting it to amount to much but *Harlequin's* editor, Barbara Frye, promptly wrote back with gushing praise and the news that she had accepted all of them for publication. Astounded by the attention, Bukowski wrote a grateful response and soon the two were corresponding regularly.

As the letters grew more personal, Frye began to complain of loneliness and bad luck in love, which she blamed on a vaguely described congenital defect in her neck. In letter after letter she bemoaned her situation and worried about ever finding a husband. Bukowski was extremely sympathetic and consoling; to the point of offering a proposal to prove she was marriage-worthy. Clearly he empathized with her physical deformity and the feeling she had that no one could ever love her. Whether he was serious or not, however, is another matter. Bukowski recalled that he was not exactly sober when he wrote the letter. Regardless, Frye took the offer to heart and soon wrote back to say she was on her way to Los Angeles. She also included photographs of herself that (depending on which source you read) either alarmed Bukowski or allayed his worst fears. Evidently, Frye was born with two vertebrae missing from her neck, leaving her chin sitting atop her sternum and preventing her from turning her head from side to side. The effect was conspicuous and a little unsettling, but in no way rendered her wholly unattractive. At least not to Bukowski, who was apparently relieved when he saw her getting off the bus in Los Angeles and attracted enough to bed her later that evening (Cherkovski wrote that Frye refused sex until they were married, but Sounes's account inspires more confidence). By Bukowski's own admission, their lovemaking was so awkward and his accuracy so poor that he failed to penetrate her or have an orgasm. They cleared up the confusion the following morning and consummated the relationship properly. Then they drove across the desert and got hitched Vegas-style. The date was October 29, 1955.

For a while they settled in Los Angeles. Bukowski was working as a shipping clerk again and they lived on that income until Barbara decided she wanted Hank to meet her family and see her hometown.

The Fryes turned out to be everything the Bukowskis were not—wealthy, successful, and respected. Great-grandfather Frye had carved himself a huge chunk of land in the last quarter of the 19th century and promptly struck oil. As if that was not enough, they also ran a successful cattle and horse-breeding operation and Barbara's cousin Jack co-founded TWA with Howard Hughes. Born eleven years after Hank to parents who would shortly divorce, Barbara had been raised by her grandparents and given a house on Frye Ranch in which to live. In addition to editing *Harlequin*, she had a good job as Wheeler court clerk.

Despite these advantages, Barbara was intent on making her own way. Marrying Bukowski offered her a ticket out and the chance to prove her independence. Most of her family disapproved of the marriage, anyway, and after a few weeks of visiting, they returned to Los Angeles to begin their new life together.

They celebrated their return by publishing a special issue of *Harlequin* that included eight poems by Bukowski. Among them was "Death Wants More Death," a perennial favorite among Bukowski fans. They also co-edited additional issues, though Bukowski apparently took advantage of his veto power and ruffled a few feathers with his heavy-handed criticism.

When it became clear that Barbara would not live off her

family's money, Bukowski went back to work in the shipping department at the Graphic Arts Center, loading boxes of writing supplies onto trucks and ducking out from time to time for a few rounds at the nearby Seven-G's bar. Barbara was unsatisfied with this career track, however, and she somehow convinced Hank that the doodles he had been making since he was a child could land him a job in advertising. Towards that end, Bukowski enrolled in an art class at City College that had him designing a Christmas ad for Texaco gas stations, but his heart was not in it and he soon dropped out again. For her part, Barbara got a clerical job at the sheriff's department. She disliked living downtown, so they moved into a house in Echo Park, a suburb to the northeast.

Tensions manifested early in Hank and Barbara's relationship—too early and too often to hope for a happy outcome. Barbara clearly had expectations for a standard of living that Bukowski did not share. Coming from a wealthy, prestigious family and believing she had married a great writer, she must have been shocked by his low class, haphazard lifestyle. Frequently, she found herself apologizing for her husband's rude behavior. Even more devastating than his economic instability or bad manners was the deconstruction of her image of him as a rebel poet about to set the world on fire.

Needless to say, the disillusionment was a two-sided affair. Bukowski quickly tired of Barbara's uppity nagging and snobbish attempts to civilize him, taking him to art galleries and such. To make matters worse, they disagreed on the subject of children. Inevitably Barbara got pregnant anyway, but she soon miscarried and both of them blamed it on Bukowski's unhealthy habits. The end came into sight when Bukowski disappointed his wife by going back to work at the post office and Barbara started incessantly talking about a man she worked with at the sheriff's office, emphasizing his class and kindness. Perhaps she was hoping to threaten Hank into changing his ways by insinuating (and perhaps initiating) an affair. If so, the plan didn't work. The couple was officially divorced on March 18, 1958. Bukowski took the '57 Plymouth he got out of the deal, drove to East Hollywood, and rented a rundown room on North Mariposa. His comfort level may have slipped a notch, but Bukowski didn't need much. A fridge full of beer, some smokes, a radio tuned to the classical station, and his "typer" was more than enough to keep him going.

As always, Bukowski turned his life into literature, bitterness fueling his forge as he hammered away at the base metals of his experience and reshaped his failed marriage into rough-hewn nuggets like "The Day I Kicked Away a Bankroll" (originally published 1959 in *Quicksilver,* later reprinted in *Run with the Hunted,* among other collections). In actuality, he was the one served with the divorce papers and not the other way around, but that fact takes little away from the visceral power the poem draws from pulling no punches and purpling no prose. One of Bukowski's greatest legacies was the obliteration of the line between "verse" and "prose." Stylistically, the vast majority of his stories and poems differ only in their typography, punctuation, and degree of conciseness. Instinctively, Bukowski knew that emotional honesty trumped flashy technique or hundred-dollar diction and that if poetry was ultimately about communicating universal feelings and ideas, then one blue-collar stanza was worth more than a thousand ivory Cantos. The trick lay in convincing everybody else.

But before he could do that, he had to find a way to work after 9:30 at night. Evidently his furious typing annoyed the neighbors and his landlord handed down a curfew that severely hamstringed a personal schedule that had him warming exactly when he was now told to cool down. Bukowski put up a fight, but in the end was forced to switch to longhand during "quiet hours."

Bukowski seldom saw his parents during his marriage to Barbara, save those times when he was in dire need of a loan. They had since moved to another house in the slightly more upscale suburb of Temple City, still inching their way along the yellow brick road of the American dream. Both would die long before they were even in eyesight of Oz, though.

Bukowski's mother went first. Collapsing under the strain of her marriage to an odious man, she evidently began to drink when Henry was away at work. It got much worse when she was diagnosed with the cancer that would eventually kill her. Bukowski first heard of her illness when she was already dying. His father allowed him to visit her only once before she died. The discrepancy over exactly what she said to him that day at the Rosemead Rest Home is good example of how small changes in a story can result in quite different characterizations. Cherkovski, basing his account no doubt on what Bukowski told him personally, wrote that Katherine finally admitted to her son that he was right; she is quoted in *Hank* as saying "Your father is a horrible man." In a poem called "cancer," Bukowski switches "terrible" for "horrible" but otherwise echoes and confirms Cherkovski's version. Sounes, on the other hand, writes that what she actually said was "Your father is a great man." A Katherine Bukowski who went to her grave in denial, still supporting her abusive husband is quite different from one who found the courage to speak her mind and console her son for his difficult upbringing. Nevertheless, the truth only mattered to Bukowski, and if he did not get what he needed from his mother in real life, he made sure to do so through his (re)writing.

Great or terrible, Henry Bukowski did not linger long over the memory of his wife of thirty-six years. Within two years of Katherine's death he was already engaged to a women who worked in a neighbor's dry-cleaning shop. As fate would have it, he never got the chance to remarry. He dropped dead in his kitchen on December 4, 1958.

Needless to say, Bukowski did not mourn his father's passing. On the contrary, he was ecstatic. He was now beholden to no one, blessedly free to do as he pleased. Still, he performed his duties as a son, making funeral arrangements and contacting everyone he thought would want to know. The list was not long. Virtually all the Bukowskis were already dead, the Fetts still in Germany. A few neighbors came, and fewer friends. The only person crying at the funeral was Henry's pitiful fiancé and it took everything Bukowski had not to slap her sensible with the truth about the man she nearly married.

Disposing of the household goods was an equally uncomfortable affair, with its standard parade of covetous neighbors laying claim to the scattered paintings, furniture, silverware, garden tools—even his mother's jars of homemade preserves. Bukowski gave it all away, happy to be rid of anything that would remind him of his father. Fact is, he got a kick out of divvying up what little booty the old man had amassed from his dogged pursuit of membership in the bourgeoisie. Still, he was not proud enough to refuse his inheritance, which, once the house was sold and the affairs settled, amounted to $15,000-$16,000. Bukowski down-played the windfall in his writings and to his friends, maintaining that it was swiftly spent to support his drinking and gambling habits, but the truth, as revealed by those closest to him, is that he socked away a little nest egg as a hedge against lean years ahead.

# CHAPTER THREE

# Outsider of the Year

*... [P]eople keep sending me poems and novels to read and collections of poesy—I mean people I have never written to or heard of—and all the stuff is bad, bad, bad. I wonder if you realize how much bad stuff is written in all earnestness? and they'll keep right on with it. thinking that they are undiscovered genius....*

—Charles Bukowski, *Screams from the Balcony*, 213

THE END OF THE '50S signaled a new beginning for Bukowski. Divorced from Barbara, with both parents dead, he was freed from the pressure to fulfill anyone's expectations of maintaining the status quo. However much he tried to ignore and defy that pressure, it had still poisoned his self-perception and kept him from truly believing that the writing life was worthwhile. In the last of the great ironies involving his father, Henry's death had provided Hank with the financial stability and emotional freedom needed to continue doing exactly what had angered and disappointed his father most. Bukowski almost certainly would have continued to write anyway, and he did not inherit enough to quit his job at the post office, but that sense of impending destitution no longer breathed down his neck.

Bukowski's desire to relinquish control to chance, if only in the short term, found its ideal outlet in his daily pilgrimages to the horse track. There he could focus on nothing but the next race—victory, defeat, happiness, despair, the whole panoply of human experience distilled to a set number of laps around a finite loop, life played out at a galloping pace. It hardly mattered that his beginner's luck had faded, replaced by the standard house odds of scattered wins and constant losses. What mattered was the thrill of the race, the exhilaration of letting go the reins and going for broke. In an article written years later for his "Notes of a Dirty Old Man" column in *Open City*, Bukowski wrote:

> I will only say this, out of a background of factories, park benches, two-bit jobs, bad women, bad weather of Life—the reason the average person is at the track is that they are driven screwy by the turn of the bolt, the foreman's insane face, the landlord's hand, the lover's dead sex, taxation, cancer, the blues; clothes that fall apart on a 3rd wearing, water that tastes like piss, doctors that run assembly-line and indecent offices, hospitals without heart, politicians with skulls filled with puss ... we can go on and on but would only be accused of being bitter and demented.... But what I am trying to tell you is, that the reason most people are at the race-track is that they are in agony, ey yeh, and they are so desperate that they will take a chance on further agony rather than face their present position...
>
> (*Notes of a Dirty Old Man*, 41)

Los Angeles may be sprawling, but like all cities it has its niches and its neighborhoods and Bukowski kept to his corner more than most. It was perhaps inevitable that he would bump into Jane again. It happened sometime in 1958, before his father died, and for the next four years or so they saw each other off and on, but the mad fire between them had been snuffed to a barely glowing pile of ash. Jane had deteriorated to such a shocking state that even Bukowski's infamously imperturbable libido was deadened by the sight of her. She had managed to survive by cleaning rooms in the seedy tenement where she lived, in lieu of paying rent, but

Bukowski sensed an even more desperate fatalism about her than before and, excepting a few dalliances for old time's sake, managed to keep his distance.

Nevertheless, he was devastated when he visited her apartment one day and found it vacated, the bedsheets soaked with blood. He heard from the landlady that an ambulance had taken her to Los Angles County Hospital. The immediate cause was a hemorrhage brought on by too much drink, but when the doctors took a closer look they found cancer in advanced stages all over her body, not to mention a cirrhotic liver on the verge of collapse. Jane was comatose when he arrived, but she did awaken once while he was there, long enough to register his presence and say "I knew it would be you." Jane died soon thereafter, on January 22, 1962.

Once again Bukowski faced the extreme unpleasantness of making funeral arrangements. He contacted Jane's businessman son in Texas, hoping he might help, but Jane had done little to endear herself and her son failed to show much emotion or concern. Bukowski did the best he could but in the end the funeral was a pathetic affair, with services cut short due to Jane's ambiguous relationship with the Catholic church.

Despite the dissolution of their love affair, Bukowski mourned Jane's death with an intensity that surprised his friends. He wept openly and went on a weeklong bender that culminated in the writing of the elegy, "For Jane, With All the Love I Had, Which Was Not Enough." Perhaps it was meeting a woman more vulnerable than himself, one of the few in his life (then or thereafter) who actually needed him more than he needed her. Perhaps a deeper love was forged in their drunken struggle for survival that no one will ever understand but them. Whatever the case, Bukowski continued to grieve and write about Jane for the rest of his life. Many of his poetry collections, particularly *The Days Run Away Like Wild Horses Over the Hills*, are filled with poems about her. She became Betty in *Post Office* and Laura in *Factotum*, and when he sat down to write *Barfly*, the screenplay based on his early years, it was Jane who got the starring role of Wanda, eventually played by Faye Dunaway.

What ultimately pulled Bukowski out the wreckage of his grief was the fact that his work was finally attracting some attention. A revolution in independent publishing was underway, with low-budget "little" magazines sprouting up all over the country, all of them searching for a new kind of writing to distinguish themselves from the establishment. Bukowski fit that bill perfectly and he fed the small presses with a never-ending stream of words. In 1959, his poems appeared in *Nomad, Coastlines, Quicksilver,* and *Epos.* And those are only the ones we know about. Bukowski's letters testify to an unknown but substantial amount of material he submitted but never saw again (he seldom made copies of his poems before sending them off). Whether any of these works made their way into publication uncredited and uncompensated is something we will probably never know for certain, given the ephemerality of the magazines in question.

When he wasn't writing poems or stories, Bukowski was writing letters—thousands of them. He maintained correspondences with a whole host of writers, editors, publishers, and friends. And they were not garden-variety letters asking after one's health, either. A letter from Bukowski was an up-to-the-minute dispatch from the front lines of a war perpetually raging, a plea for help and a howl of rage, leavened here and there with dirty talk and sarcasm. No less than five volumes of his correspondence have found their way to print and any fan or researcher who overlooks them is missing out on the richest resource available for understanding the man behind the myth.

In addition to exposing a less guarded and more self-questioning side than he allowed be seen in his fiction and poetry, all this letter writing helped Bukowski develop strong relationships with the kind of people who could get his work into print. One of the first to take up the cause was E.V. Griffith, editor of *Hearse* magazine. Griffith published two broadsides by Bukowski and then set about producing *Flower, Fist and Bestial Wail,* Buk's debut collection and *Hearse* Chapbook Number 5. The project was plagued by delays that nearly sent Bukowski into a tailspin of depression and frustration. In one letter to the editor, he even threatened to go public with the "whole history of this notorious and impossible chapbook nightmare" (*Screams,* 24). But when the finished product arrived in the mail a week later (October 14,

1960), Bukowski was so mortified and grateful that he dashed off another letter. This time he was effusive with his praise and closed with contrition: "I hope I can live down any disgust I have caused you" (*Screams*, 25).

Other friends and supporters at the time included Evelyn Thorne, editor of *Epos* magazine, which devoted a special issue to Bukowski in March of 1962 called *Poems and Drawings*; the editors at *Targets* magazine, who, from 1960-1961, published two entire signatures of his poetry, including the much-loved "Tragedy of the Leaves"; Carl Larsen, a fellow poet and editor who issued Bukowski's second chapbook, *Longshot Pomes for Broke Players* (early 1962); and R.R. Cuscaden, editor of *Midwest* magazine and publisher of another Bukowski chapbook called *Run with the Hunted* (March 1962). Cuscaden was also the first to write an analytical essay on Bukowski's work, called "Charles Bukowski: Poet in a Ruined Landscape" and printed in the spring-summer 1962 issue of *Satis*. Other supportive essays soon followed, including "Charles Bukowski and the Savage Surfaces" by Louisiana State University English professor and Bukowski pen pal John William Corrington (*North West Review*, 1963).

Individually, these appearances in the small press exposed Bukowski to a small group of readers, but collectively they kicked off his career and gave him the confidence needed to continue with his work. Although great fans of his poetry, none of the editors mentioned above were prepared at the time to devote all their energies exclusively to Bukowski. That distinction belongs to Jon and Gypsy Lou Webb.

Jon Edgar Webb was a curious mix of literature aficionado, gentle outlaw, and blue-collar workingman. A grammar school teacher in early adulthood who went on to become a police reporter for the *Cleveland Plain Dealer* and other large newspapers, Webb also wrote short fiction and developed acquaintances with some major literary figures, like Hemingway and Sherwood Anderson. In 1930, Webb's life took a strange turn when he was arrested for the armed robbery of a jewelry store and sent to a reformatory for three years. While inside, he produced a prison newspaper and learned the basics of typesetting. A few years after he was released, Jon met and wed an Italian woman named Louise whose colorful clothes and long black hair had earned her the nickname of Gypsy Lou. Together they moved to New Orleans and founded Loujon Press in the cramped basement apartment (and former slave quarters) of a crumbling French Quarter manse. Their first major undertaking was issue number one of a new literary magazine they dubbed *The Outsider*, which appeared in the fall of 1961. Two years in the making, it was painstakingly printed on quality stock using an obsolete letterpress and featured poems and prose by the rising stars of avant-garde literature: Henry Miller, William Burroughs, Gregory Corso, Gary Snyder, Allen Ginsberg, and Lawrence Ferlinghetti. Surprisingly, given the cultural cachet of those forenamed, the issue's centerpiece and largest share of ink was devoted to eleven poems by Bukowski, whose work had been introduced to the Webbs by Jory Sherman, a poet friend of Bukowski's and the Webb's West Coast editor. Jon and Gypsy Lou fell instantly in love with the honesty and earthiness of Bukowski's verse and became dead set on becoming his main publisher.

The Webbs distinguished themselves not only by making attractive, award-winning publications by hand but also with their keen editorial eyes. Only the best of Bukowski's work was selected, such as his early effort "old man, dead in a room," and this helped the poet a great deal, for his output was as uneven as it was prolific. Two more of his poems were selected for the second issue of *The Outsider* (published in the summer of 1962), but the third issue (spring 1963) focused almost exclusively on his work and even featured a photo of his pockmarked mug on the cover. The Webbs also gave Buk the "Outsider of the Year Award" for 1962, as well as a Loujon Press Award, which carried the prize of a full-length collection devoted exclusively to his work.

Bukowski struggled over a title for a while before settling on a line from a poem by his personal favorite, Robinson Jeffers. *It Catches My Heart in Its Hands: New and Selected Poems 1955-1963*, Gypsy Lou Series no. 1, was eventually released October 1963, in 777 glorious copies. The Webbs attended lovingly, almost slavishly, to everything they published and Bukowski's first true volume of verse was no exception. According to the book's colophon (a wonderful read in and of itself), nine different colors of *Linweave Spectra* paper were handfed, one page at a time, into their "ancient 8 by 12 Chandler and Price letterpress." (Krumhansl, 23) The colophon goes on to record all the trials and tribulations of the book's creation, from rainwater seeping into the pages to a whole menagerie of local critters causing havoc with the ink and type. It was clearly a labor of love. John William Corrington was enlisted to write an introduction, and hundreds of pages were sent to Bukowski to sign. The result spoke for itself, but Bukowski was too overjoyed to contain his admiration and gratitude. In one letter to the Webbs, written on the day he first spied the finished product, he said, "by god, you've done it, you've done it, and I'm proud and struck and awed that you have—the both of you—caught me up in it." In a second letter, written later that day as he continued to savor the book over a few beers and a cigar, he wrote, "the miracle is yours; you have drowned me in honor, and no matter what cheap hotel, what jail, what grave is there for me, they can never take away the miracle" (*Screams*, 93–94). These days, copies of *It Catches* easily fetch thousands of dollars, if they can be found at all.

While that project was still taking shape, Bukowski began an affair with a woman who had written him earlier in the year to express her enthusiasm for his poetry. Her given name was Frances Elizabeth Dean, but she ultimately changed it to FrancEyE. Born in San Rafael, California, she later moved to Massachusetts after her father died, and was raised by her paternal grandparents. She studied and wrote poetry at Smith College, and began corresponding with other poets after graduating, one of whom showed her some of Bukowski's work several years later, after she had married a soldier and given birth to four daughters. Her marriage ended sometime thereafter and she moved across the country to be with her mother in Garden Grove, near Los Angeles. Both she and Bukowski were feeling down and out at the time, he over Jane's death and FrancEyE over her divorce and separation from her children. This desperation, coupled with her desire to meet the man whose work she so admired, helps explain why she was willing to walk several miles, take a bus, and then hail a cab in the middle of the night to console Bukowski after he finally called her one drunken evening and demanded that she come over. When FrancEyE arrived, they sat up and talked to each other through the wee hours of the morning, finding consolation in each other's misery. The next day they went to the horse races together and soon they were inseparable. With no money to speak of, FrancEyE even rented a room in Los Angeles, just to be closer to him.

In retrospect, it is clear that she invested more into the relationship than he did, learning to accept his drinking, his gambling, and his foul turns of temper despite her strong distaste for all these things. Bukowski would later disparage her looks, and her liberal beliefs, but he badmouthed almost all his lovers and friends and there is no questioning that his reaction to what happened next suggests at least some degree of emotional investment.

Bukowski worried constantly about getting FrancEyE pregnant and warned her often that he was entirely against the idea of having children, but that is exactly what happened towards the end of 1963. FrancEyE didn't tell him at first, while she considered an abortion, but in the end she decided to have the baby with or without him. Bukowski took the news as best as could be expected and even proposed marriage, but FrancEyE declined, having long before soured on the institution. Instead, they moved into a bungalow together on De Longpre Ave, in East Hollywood. Despite the dinginess of his old apartment, and the terrible neighbors, Bukowski had fond feelings for the place and all the writing he had done there, as evidenced by a letter to the Webbs, written May 1, 1964, in which he says "Old 1623 is gone and it was a magic number and magic place" before launching into a tirade about the nitpicking landlords (*Screams*, 107).

Their new landlords proved to be much more accommodating. Beyond overlooking their unmarried status (a real stigma and deal-killer in those days), Francis and Grace Crotty were also known to supply their tenants with whiskey, beer, and dented tins of food to help them through lean times. More importantly, Bukowski could type whenever he pleased without worrying about downstairs neighbors banging on the floor with their broomsticks.

As with his marriage to Barbara, differences in personality, habit, and philosophy were soon causing problems in Hank and FrancEyE's relationship. As the pressure of impending fatherhood grew, Bukowski began drinking to excess more often and openly criticized everything that defined FrancEyE, from her progressive social beliefs to the poetry workshops she attended and the friends she made there. Once he even questioned his paternity of the child she was carrying, in front of her, to his friend Jory Sherman. FrancEyE knew it was just typical Bukowski machismo, but that didn't soften the hurt very much. They were headed for a split, and both of them knew it, but with the baby on the way they somehow managed to keep it together.

One happy distraction came in the form of an extended visit from Jon and Gypsy Lou. The couple made the long trip from New Orleans to finally meet the man behind the words that had inspired such devotion in them. They were also there to discuss his next volume of verse. Bukowski felt they had plenty of material to choose from already, and that they should consider putting out a less lavish production to speed things along. The Webbs, however, held true to their standards and argued that they had already selected the print-worthy poems from his voluminous submissions and more quality work was needed if they were going to invest their time and money in another collection. But beyond these editorial quibbles, their visit was suffused with mutual admiration, affection, and relief that they got along as well in person as they did on the page. The Webbs returned to New Orleans re-invigorated and eager to read what came out of Buk's "typer" next.

Several weeks later, on September 7, 1964, Marina Louise Bukowski was born, her middle name a heartfelt tribute to Gypsy Lou. At first, Hank was nervous about his ability to be a good father, but all that worry melted away when he found himself holding her and FrancEyE testified years later (despite numerous reasons to want to say otherwise) that he was indeed a loving and attentive caretaker, taking on many of the responsibilities that other men were shirking during that era, like changing Marina's diapers and feeding her.

Bukowski was working nights at the time, 6:30 p.m.–2:30 a.m., at a massive mail sorting facility ominously called the Terminal Annex, like something out of a Terry Gilliam movie. He and hundreds of coworkers staffed a giant work floor futilely attempting to keep up with the never-ending flow of incoming mail. The work was repetitive and mindless, the din of the machinery deafening, the production expectations of his superiors draconian. Before long it began to take a serious physical toll on him. His back and shoulders ached constantly. His morale slipped and his surliness surfaced more and more often. For a while, he somehow continued to find time to write despite the hardships, not to mention a new baby and constant visits from friends and admirers. But inevitably his output slowed. Tensions between Hank and FrancEyE continued to mount as he drank himself ugly and uncorked his frustration all over her. To make matters worse, Jon Webb was constantly asking for more poems for the new collection. FrancEyE took Marina to Washington, D.C. for a visit with the daughters from her previous marriage, but that was just a temporary measure. After talking it over with the Webbs, Bukowski decided a break from everything was required to focus his mind on writing, so in March of 1965 he boarded a train out of Union Station to New Orleans.

According to Gypsy Lou, he was drunk on arrival and just kept on drinking when they got to their place in the French Quarter, where he found pages and pages of his work piled chest high and squirreled into every corner. The Webbs put him up in the house of a friend named Minnie Segate, who cooked and cleaned for him while he was there, happy at first just to be near the great Charles Bukowski. The Webbs had also asked a New York artist named Noel Rockmore, newly transplanted to the Crescent City, to design etchings for the cover and some interior illustrations. He and Bukowski hit it off and drank together for a few nights, causing havoc and upsetting Minnie before Jon Webb finally drew the line and told Bukowski to get cracking. A letter written at the time to a poet friend in Canada named Al Purdy (their complete correspondence has since been published as *The Bukowski/Purdy Letters*) shows that Bukowski was perfectly aware of the damage his drinking caused and yet refused like a stubborn child to do much about it:

> This won't be much of a letter. Sick, sick, sitting here shaking & frightened & cowardly & depressed. I have hurt almost everybody's feelings. I am not a very good drunk. And it's the same when I awaken here as anywhere. I only want sweet peace and kindliness when I awaken—but there's always some finger pointing, telling me some terrible deed I committed during the night. It seems I make a lot of mistakes and it seems that I am not allowed any. The finger used to belong to my father, or to some shack-job, and now it's an editor's finger. But it's the same. For Christ's sake, Al, I don't understand people, never will. It looks like I got to travel pretty much alone.
>
> (*Screams*, 136)

But once again Bukowski proved he could hunker down and produce when he put his mind to it. Chastised by the Webbs, he sat in Minnie's house and wrote poem after poem, sometimes as many as fifteen a day. If he did not have any new verses with him when he went to visit the Webbs, then he was not allowed inside. One by one the poems were read, judged, and either discarded outright or fed immediately into the Webb's letterpress. Jon and Gypsy Lou drove themselves as hard as they did Bukowski, working twelve-hour days to keep the pages coming. Gradually the book took shape. They argued over the title—if there was one thing Bukowski had plenty of, it was ideas for titles—but in the end the Webbs won out and *Crucifix in a Deathhand* was born.

Jon and Gypsy Lou did sanction one diversion during Bukowski's visit, but it turned out to be a very bad idea. Early fan and supporter John William Corrington wanted to meet his literary hero and so the Webbs organized a get-together with a few other friends. Corrington was very much the academic—he had just earned his doctorate, published his first novel, and was teaching English at Louisiana State University. Bukowski disparaged all academics, partly because he felt unlearned in their company and partly because he believed faculty life ruined good writers, but until that point he had treated Corrington with respect, largely because Corrington flattered his ego and helped his career. But in person, with a bunch of beers in him, Bukowski became confrontational and offensive, and, not for the first or last time, permanently alienated someone who had done him a great deal of good.

*Crucifix in a Deathhand* was published a few weeks later—3,100 copies delivered as they were completed, most of which Bukowski signed by hand. Several dozen deluxe editions included letters, drawings, and special inscriptions by Bukowski in addition to the four Rockmore etchings that graced the standard editions. Once again, the Webbs had created an instant collector's item. More importantly, at least as far as Bukowski was concerned, they widened his readership. Lyle Stuart, a New York publisher, agreed to handle and finance the distribution. Bukowski was thrilled when Jon Webb wrote to say Henry Miller had praised it, but deep down he worried that his rush-job, assembly-line method of composition had resulted in a weaker effort overall and many of his friends agreed. A letter written later that summer reads:

> I am sorry; mostly I only write poems, and many of these—as you know—not so good. [William] Wantling tells me this and you tell me this about Crucifix, and I know that it is true. I knew that when I went down there in New Orleans, I knew I sensed that old man Webb wanted more and better poems but I couldn't do it. I just kept wandering the streets a drunken jackal of self, wandering drunk, and I could not come up with it.
>
> (*Screams*, 195)

Bukowski also feared that some would see an incongruity between the down-and-out image Bukowski advertised in the poems and the extraordinary production values of the book itself, which sold for a princely $7.50. Regardless of the quality of the paper it was printed on, Bukowski did stay true to form and, if anything, *Crucifix* displayed an even leaner, sparer Bukowski than before, a style that presaged much of the work to come. Whether that made the book better or worse than *It Catches* remains open to debate.

Like most writers, Bukowski's opinion of his own work went through rapid fluctuations. Shortly after the publication of *Crucifix*, Jay Nash and Ron Offen of *Chicago Literary Times* contacted Bukowski and offered to put out another chapbook under their Cyofeth Publications imprint. Bukowski agreed, on the condition that *he* select the works. In an act of authorial defiance, he chose poems rejected from previous volumes (particularly *It Catches* and *Crucifix*), entitled the book *Cold Dogs in the Courtyard*, and wrote an introduction awash in a new wave of self-confidence just a few months after his doubt over *Crucifix*. It reads in part:

> I have never selected my own work for collection, feeling—as the formula goes—that a writer is not a very good judge of his own work ... Very lately, I can tell a good woman when I see one, a good fire, a good whiskey, a good car, a good painting ... why couldn't I tell a good poem? Even one of my own. So, I went though the magazines looking ...
>
> (Cherkovski, 154)

Bukowski closed the intro with a parting shot at his previous publishers: "And Jon, Rob, Carl, E.V. I forgive you, this time."

The individual or individuals to whom he was writing often conditioned whether Bukowski came on with a swaggering bluster or a more honest humility. What he admitted in private correspondence, and what he broadcast to his readers, were often very different. The letter quoted above, in which Bukowski accepts implied criticism of *Crucifix*, was written to Douglas Blazek, a young poet and underground publisher whose opinion Bukowski clearly valued. Blazek was the man behind *Ole*, another influential little magazine that Bukowski helped launch, but unlike *The Outsider*, *Ole* heralded the coming of the zines—irreverent rags published in slapdash fashion with a mimeograph machine. Blazek and Bukowski corresponded regularly throughout the '60s, starting when the former accepted three poems by the latter for the first issue of *Ole*. Despite their difference in age (Blazek was born twenty years later) the two writers shared a lot in common. As a teenager, Blazek had his own terrible bout with acne and identified himself as an outcast. He also worked hard hours in a foundry, ducked mainstream political issues, and believed poetry needed to be rescued from the ivory tower.

Blazek was also responsible for getting Bukowski to write prose again. After hearing about Hank's early efforts at short fiction, he asked for something along those lines for *Ole*. Instead of a story, per se, Bukowski delivered a kind of manifesto called "A Rambling Essay On Poetics And The Bleeding Life Written While Drinking a Six Pack (Tall)." In it, Bukowski perpetuated his own growing legend by spinning a number of white lies that made him sound even more crazy and heroic than he really was. He also threw down the gauntlet and spit in the face of academia, appraising the Canon of accumulated literature as essentially worthless to him, and by extension the average human. The response among readers was tremendous, generating a flood of fan mail.

Blazek knew he was on to something. In August, 1965, he followed up on the success of "A Rambling Essay" by publishing a standalone chapbook of another prose work by Bukowski entitled *Confessions of a Man Insane Enough to Live with Beasts*. Comprised of nine shorter pieces recounting Hank's troubled upbringing and early adulthood, this seminal work heralded the first appearance of Henry Chinaski, the autobiographical protagonist destined to feature in five of his six novels and an untold number of poems. In early 1966, Bukowski again plumbed the lower reaches of his real-world experience with *All the Assholes in the World and Mine*, a rip-roaring write-up of a recent operation to alleviate his notoriously bad case of hemorrhoids, which Blazek published under his Open Skull imprint. (While the essay was a success, apparently the operation was not, for visitors often made note of the empty tubes of Preparation H that constantly littered Bukowski's bathroom.)

Bukowski and Blazek soon acquired allies in their quest to shake up the literary world. On the one hand, closely investigating many of these collaborations and associations can help rescue Bukowski from the kind of monolithic cult of personality that would have us believe in all his tough-guy posturing and claims to artistic sovereignty. They also belie the notion, oft espoused by Bukowski during his lifetime and later by Bukowski purists furthering their own agendas, that he had no time for liberals, Beats, academics, or homosexuals. On the other hand, the antagonistic dissolution of many of these relationships strongly suggests Bukowski's only true allegiance was to himself. Although there were others (John Martin's unparalleled impact is covered in the next chapter and John William Corrington's influence has already been mentioned), the six most noteworthy of these sometimes-tenuous friendships were with William Wantling, Steve Richmond, John Bryan, Harold Norse, Sheri Martinelli, and Carl Weissner.

Mentioned alongside Blazek in the aforementioned letter of self-doubt, William Wantling was another of Bukowski's pen pals and an occasional confidante, someone he respected and even admired for a time. Wantling's background as a marine, ex-con, and survivor of San Quentin State Prison gave him special status among the outlaw poets and his raw, angry poems were published almost as widely as Bukowski's. When Buk and Neeli Cherkovski established their own magazine in 1969, Wantling was among the select few whose work was chosen for inclusion. As time went on, however, Wantling's prolonged drug and alcohol addiction stole some of the fire from his writing and Bukowski began to lose his regard for him, especially when Wantling accepted a teaching position at a college in Illinois. The sad end to the tale of their friendship, recounted in Chapter Five, marks one of Bukowski's lowest moments as a human being.

Steve Richmond was also an upstart young poet with an urge to upset the establishment. Bukowski's poem "freedom" in issue number one of Blazek's *Ole* magazine hit Richmond like a neutron bomb—he would later dub it the strongest piece of writing he had ever read. A law school graduate-cum-hippie who dropped acid and hung out with Jim Morrison at UCLA, Richmond used his upper middle class family's money to open a radical bookshop where he sold Bukowski chapbooks, among others, and published a magazine called *The Earth Rose*. The first issue's outrageous headline ("Fuck Hate") was followed by an equally incendiary mission statement that earned Richmond a charge of obscenity and resulted in some of his stock being seized by the local authorities.

Bukowski and Richmond continued to interact, correspond, and collaborate throughout the '60s but had a falling out in the early '70s when Bukowski penned a piece called "300 Poems" that satirized Richmond's soft lifestyle and mediocre poems. However, various biographers and commentators have exaggerated both the supposed disdain behind the poem and the resultant estrangement between them—two years after *Mockingbird*, Bukowski dedicated *Burning in Water Drowning in Flame* to Richmond. Early that same year he gave this assessment of Richmond in a letter to editor A.D. Winans: "Steve ... knows how to write a *sentence* ... I have said for years that Steve Richmond is the most underrated human and writer and painter that I know" (Bukowski, *Living on Luck*, 187). Over a decade later Richmond was among the few friends from the old days that Bukowski invited to the reception after his marriage to Linda Lee Beighle. Richmond's own, somewhat scatterbrained, take on their relationship can be found in his book, *Spinning off Bukowski*, published in 1996 by Sun Dog Press. Among the randomly organized impressions and vivid recollections of his literary hero, their first meeting in 1965 stands out as particularly revealing. Upon first entering Bukowski's inner sanctum on De Longpre, Richmond was transfixed by the sight of Bukowski's desk, which, in contrast to the mess that surrounded it, was a paragon of orderliness and professionalism, dominated by a massive, pigeon-holed shelving unit that he used to organize his vast array of writing supplies. The metaphor was clear to Richmond—live however you want, but approach your trade with serious intent.

John Bryan was even more of a hippie than Richmond, someone who not only ingested copious amounts of psychedelics but spent a great deal of time and energy in the early sixties evangelizing their social benefits. On first blush, this made him an extremely unlikely Bukowski confederate, but Buk was not as old school as he portrayed himself to be. While it is true he had no patience for muddle-headed liberal philosophy or social activism (especially when promulgated by rich white kids who had not suffered a day in their lives), Bukowski was not above smoking marijuana or taking pills to alter his mood. And according to John

Thomas, another close friend at the time met through Bryan, Buk did take acid at least once. Thomas recounts this and other hilarious tales of his time with Bukowski in *Bukowski in the Bathtub*. But beyond his recreational drug use, there was a simpler, and more pertinent, rationale for Bukowski's willingness to compromise some of his personal antipathies and associate with flaming liberals like John Bryan—Bryan wanted to publish his writing. Initially, Bryan did so in a little magazine called *Renaissance* that he published out of San Francisco from 1961–1963. Sometime in 1964–1965 Bryan moved down to Los Angeles to take over the editorship of the L.A. Free Press and resurrected *Renaissance* under the new name *Notes from Underground*. Bukowski appeared in both versions of the magazine. A few years later, Bryan would be instrumental in securing Bukowski his largest readership to date, by way of his underground newspaper *Open City*.

Wantling, Richmond, and Bryan were younger than Bukowski and part of a markedly different generation. Wantling and Richmond idolized him as the figurehead of a literary movement in which they wanted membership. Bryan may not have cared for his politics or cantankerousness, but he certainly coveted his readership draw. Bukowski's relationship with Harold Norse, however, was the complete inverse of that—Norse was a contemporary and hailed from a realm of literary respectability to which Bukowski secretly aspired. At 22, Norse was befriended by and apprenticed to W.H. Auden. In 1951, he began a ten-year correspondence and close relationship with William Carlos Williams, who dubbed Norse the best poet of his generation. From 1960–1963, Norse lived in the infamous "Beat Hotel" in Paris with William Burroughs, Allen Ginsberg, and Gregory Corso, among others. His experimental novel about the period, *Beat Hotel,* was published in 1973 and remains one of the genre's seminal works. A collection of poems, *Hotel Nirvana,* was published a year later and nominated for the National Book Award. Despite all this success, Norse never attained the kind of fame and celebrity that, in Bukowski's opinion, diluted whatever artistic triumphs Kerouac and Ginsberg managed to achieve. He also avoided politicizing his homosexuality, something for which Bukowski had no tolerance whatsoever. When Bukowski first contacted Norse in 1963 (through Kay Johnson, a fellow denizen of the "Beat Hotel"), Norse's work was consistently appearing in an extremely influential and well-respected periodical called the *Evergreen Review* that was among the first to publish the Beats alongside their Absurdist cohorts in Europe (Samuel Beckett, Gene Genet, Alexander Trocchi, et al.). Because it rode the razor's edge of academic acceptance, *Evergreen* represented for Bukowski a kind of loophole into the canon of serious literature, through which he might gain entrance without having to compromise his vociferously stated anti-intellectualism. The only problem was, *Evergreen* kept rejecting Bukowski's submissions. But when Norse recommended him, *Everygreen* promptly accepted. Thus, in addition to a simple love of his work, Bukowski had good reason for holding Norse in higher regard than any other writer with whom he regularly corresponded. He called Norse the "Prince of Poets" and in one letter, Bukowski wrote:

> Old William C. Williams knew a poet when he saw one. I wish I could use language like you. You have all the words and you use them exactly ... I don't have the words, I am afraid of them. I work with black and white and dirty stick.

Bukowski's false modesty aside, the respect was mutual. Norse likened getting letters from Bukowski to "corresponding with Van Gogh. His use of language conjured up in my mind, the mad Dutchman's use of paint, like a force of nature." And when Norse was offered a deal in 1968 with Penguin Books, to put out a collection of his verse, he told poetry editor Nikos Stangos he would rather be published in their better-selling series of three-poet books and then nominated Bukowski and Philip Lamantia as his preferred company. The resulting collection, *Penguin Modern Poets No. 13*, was published in 1969 and garnered Bukowski his first mainstream critical success and an international readership.

Both of the quotes cited above were taken from "Laughter in Hell," Norse's contribution to *Drinking with Bukowski: Recollections of the Poet Laureate of Skid Row* (94–95). In this warm and elegiac essay, filled with regret over the atrophy of their friendship, Norse also drops hints about the forthcoming publication of his vast correspondence with Bukowski. No doubt this treasure trove of new material will reveal even more about his old friend's complicated need for acceptance from his peers, not to mention Norse's controversial assertion that old Buk was a closet bisexual.

Sherri Martinelli provided another of Bukowski's tangential brushes with the rarified world of high art and literature. Despite a seven-year correspondence sizeable enough to fill a three-hundred-page book (*Beerspit and Night Cursing: The Correspondence of Charles Bukowski and Sheri Martinelli 1960–1967*), their interaction remains one of the least written about aspects of this period in Bukowski's life. She merited no mention in either the Sounes or Cherkovski books, most likely because their letters were still unpublished at the time those books were written and Bukowski, hurt by her criticisms, often badmouthed her in his other correspondence. Though a full evaluation of what these letters and Bukowski and Martinelli's relationship say about Bukowski's equivocal stance towards fellow poets and their poetics remains outside the scope of this volume, a few remarks do seem in order.

Martinelli was a classic example of someone fated to languish in the shadow of the leading lights with which she surrounded herself. After becoming a member of Anais Nin's inner circle (Martinelli is mentioned several times in Nin's *Diary*), she also acted in an experimental film by the groundbreaking director Maya Deren; fraternized with Charlie Parker and other jazz greats; befriended and counseled many of the Beats, particularly Allen Ginsberg; and modeled for photographers Karl Bissinger and Cliff Wolfe, among others. A passel of writers, from the poet H. D. to novelists as dissimilar as William Gaddis and Larry McMurtry, used her as the basis for fictional characters or subjects of their writing. Still others, like E.E. Cummings, appreciated and collected her artwork. But the name with which she will be forever associated (when she is mentioned at all) is Ezra Pound. Martinelli became his muse and lover while Pound was confined to St. Elizabeth's mental hospital after pleading insanity to treason charges during World War II. Pound subsequently immortalized her as

"Sibylla," "Undine," and other mythological figures in his later verses, particularly Cantos 90–95 (*Beerspit and Night Cursing*, 11–23)

Pound abandoned Martinelli shortly before his release from St. Elizabeth's in 1958, and she spent the next couple years living in Mexico before settling in San Francisco, where she founded a magazine called the *Anagogic & Paideumic Review*. Bukowski submitted poems to the magazine sometime during the first half of 1960 and received a rejection letter from Martinelli for his troubles, kicking off an extended epistolary boxing match.

These letters should dispel, once and for all, the illusion that Bukowski was uncultured and poorly read outside his own small sphere of literary predilections. Though he generally hated intellectual chit-chat and could be viciously supercilious towards those whose opinions he felt were generated by trends or borrowed ideas, he did enjoy arguing over the merits of various writers, as well as defending his own aesthetics, with certain individuals. Sherri Martinelli was one of them. At first, this probably had more to do with her close association with Ezra Pound than any desperate desire on his part to be published in her magazine, but as the correspondence continued, he recognized Martinelli as an original thinker and one of the more intelligent women he had ever met ("You are lit by enough flames to burn us all" he wrote to her in 1963, *Beerspit*, 295). While they were diametrically opposed in their philosophy towards literature—Bukowski devalued the classics and felt writing was a purely personal endeavor, while Martinelli (following Pound's edicts) considered the history of art to be nothing less than the blueprint for civilization—they shared the same degree of idiosyncrasy in their writing styles. Martinelli abbreviated a lot of her words and often used dialect, Bukowski was a sloppy typist and poor speller (though some of it was intentional), and both of them wrote when they drank, used unorthodox punctuation, and expressed themselves in fragmentary fashion (*Beerspit*, 28–31). Reading their correspondence is thus rather like eavesdropping on the encoded communiqués of double agents in opposite camps of some secret war over the meaning of art.

Ultimately, they both were too entrenched in their opinions to defect, and Bukowski grew increasingly more irritated by Martinelli's high-handed criticism. For her part, Martinelli did not enjoy the unflattering and invasive treatment she sometimes received in his writings (e.g., *Wormwood Review* editor Marvin Malone once printed a letter from Bukowski in response to his request for instructions on sending out contributor's copies that contained the following [note the inversion of Martinelli's initials]: "well, ya better mail one to M.S. or she'll prob. put her pisser in the over, she thinks she is a goddess, and maybe she is, I sure as hell w[oul]d[n]'t know," (*Screams*, 35)). They never met in person, and evidently their correspondence was terminated by an April 1967 letter in which Bukowski, prodded by his friend John Thomas, accused Martinelli of lying about her relationship with Pound.

Not all of Bukowsk's correspondences and collaborations ended badly. A rare few lasted for the rest of his life, especially when contact was limited to letters, business dealings, and the occasional visit. A perfect example is his relationship with his German translator and agent, Carl Weissner.

Weissner was a university graduate student bored to death by a literature curriculum still steeped in the classics. He was first exposed to American culture by the black GIs living in his town after the war, who hipped him to jazz and the new slang then in vogue (in *Hollywood*, Bukowski's fourth novel, he depicts Weissner as still using this ghetto lingo nearly twenty-five years later). Like many young European intellectuals in the '60s, Weissner was captivated by the wave of new writing coming out of the States (or from Americans living abroad). Kerouac's *On the Road* touched a major nerve and soon he was reading Burroughs and Miller—everything he could get his hands on that spoke to his love of the experimental and the anti-traditional. Of particular interest was the "cut-up" technique employed by Burroughs, Norse, and fellow Beat Hotel guest Brion Gysin, whereby single words or chunks of discovered text were spliced together in random fashion to create thought-collages and unexpected word patterns (the technique was also used with sounds and film segments).

Inspired by the example being set in the States, Weissner established his own alternative magazine, naming it *Klactoveedsedsteen* after a tune by bebop sax genius Charlie Parker. But instead of simply serving as the German mouthpiece for the American avant-garde, *Klacto* was one of the first periodicals to tap into what had become a truly worldwide movement, enlisting submissions from Mexico City, Calcutta, and everywhere in between. Weissner first came across Bukowski in 1966, when he read six poems published in a recent issue of the English magazine, *Iconoature*. His reaction was as immediate and compelling as that of Jon Webb, FrancEyE, and all the others. After tracking down his address, Weissner wrote to Bukowski and promptly received one of Buk's trademark letters, full of honesty and barebones humanity. The young German was hooked. He felt certain he would not be alone among his fellow Germans in his appreciation and began making plans to introduce his country to Bukowski's brand of writing.

In the meantime, Weissner landed a Fulbright fellowship to go to New York and write a thesis on the poet Charles Olson. After discovering others were already at work on the same thing, he shifted gears and engaged in a number of literary projects, all the while planning to somehow get out to California and meet Bukowski.

Weissner got his chance in the summer of 1968. Bukowski was supposed to pick him up at the airport, but unsurprisingly he flaked and Weissner had to find his own way by bus. (A decade later, Bukowski admitted in a letter to Weissner that, having never traveled by plane, he was simply too intimidated by the airport to come pick him up.) Weisnner discovered a note on the door from Buk when he arrived at 5134 De Longpre, telling him to go on in and wait. He entered the bungalow and soaked up the sights and smells of Bukowski's lair, examining the bookcases overflowing with periodicals Bukowski had appeared in and the Remington "typer" on which he worked, until the man himself showed up with a six pack of beer and apology. Weissner hung on every word and filed them away for an introduction he would write years later to a bestselling collection of Bukowski poems that he would also edit and translate. It was the beginning of a long and profitable friendship for Bukowski, one that ultimately led to a triumphant return to the town of his birth. But that was still a decade away, and one of the main players in the unfolding drama of Bukowski's career remains to be introduced. To do that, we must first backtrack a little, to the fall of 1965.

# CHAPTER FOUR

# A Little Bird Comes Calling

*When the crowd quieted down, Hank cleared his
throat and took a long swig of beer. "Okay. Let's
begin this thing," he said. His cool, methodical, res-
onant voice filled the room. He had command, and
remained in control throughout the long reading,
never missing a beat.*

—Neeli Cherkovski, *Bukowski: A Life*

AS ANTISOCIAL AND ORNERY as Bukowski could be in person,
something in his writing kept inspiring people to seek him out.
Most simply wanted to rub elbows and share a drink with the
"skid row genius," but a few genuinely tried to help him garner
the literary reputation, if not financial remuneration, they felt he
deserved. Jon and Gypsy Lou Webb were very instrumental in
lighting that spark; Blazek, Bryan, Weissner, et al. kept it flick-
ering in their respective corners of the underground; but the
man responsible for lighting a signal fire for all the world to see
was an unassuming book collector and businessman named John
Martin.

In 1965, Martin still managed an office supply company and
spent his spare time tending to his enviable collection of modern

first editions. He had dreams of running his own press, but little idea where to begin.

One day Martin picked up a copy of *The Outsider* and read something by Bukowski that made an instant and lasting impact. He promptly tracked down copies of *It Catches My Heart in Its Hands* and *Crucifix in a Deathhand*, then contacted Bukowski himself for copies of the early chapbooks. Quickly devoured, all of this material only deepened the impression that he had happened upon America's greatest undiscovered poet. He could hardly believe such a talent had been relegated to underground obscurity and, as his inclination to build a small press began to harden into serious intention, he wondered whether Bukowski might be the keystone.

Martin wrote to Bukowski again in the fall of 1965 to request a meeting, but Hank was too busy at the time finding a new place for FrancEye and Marina to live (by that time it was clear to both of them that their relationship was doomed and the split was, if not exactly amicable, at least consensual). Martin wrote again after the holidays and suggested he bring by some bottles of liquor that had been given to him by friends who were unaware he did not drink. This time, the offer of booze seemed to get Bukowski's attention and Martin was given the ok to stop by for a visit (Sounes, 78).

Like most of Bukowski's admirers, Martin had created his own mental picture of him as a noble hero toiling away in the anonymous dignity of some quiet room somewhere. When he actually met the man face to face, registered his Frankenstein features, and found him drinking alone amid the pigsty squalor left in the wake of FrancEye's departure, he wondered whether he might have made a mistake. Bukowski offered him a beer, but Martin reiterated that he didn't drink. Normally, that fact alone would have been enough to turn off Bukowski, but something in his visitor's professional bearing and flattering enthusiasm told him to reserve judgment. Martin asked if Bukowski had any unpublished material lying around that he might have a look at and Bukowski directed him to a closet practically overflowing with pages. For Martin, it was like discovering King Tut's tomb—an almost unimaginable amount of literary treasure just waiting for him to plunder. He picked up a few pages at random and was so impressed by what he read that he offered then and there to publish a few broadsides. He explained his plan to establish a small press dedicated exclusively to contemporary poetry and his hope that Bukowski might become his star author. Needless to say, Bukowski liked what he heard, saw a potentially lucrative partner in Martin, and agreed to let him take whatever he wanted. Up to that point he had made almost no money from his writing—most of his publishers, including Jon Webb, paid him in contributor copies, if at all, so he had virtually nothing to lose.

In the end, Martin chose five poems from Bukowski's backlog and published thirty copies of each. He dubbed his new venture Black Sparrow Press, after a line from a William Carlos Williams poem. Initially, Phil Klein, who also did the printing for Martin's office supply company, handled the design and layout duties. Later, Martin's wife Barbara took over and was responsible for the trademark look of Black Sparrow's books, praised the world over for their simple elegance and no-nonsense typography.

The first of the broadsides, a grim piece about a man's self-castration called *True Story*, appeared in April 1966. Three more followed, one per month, for the next three months: *On Going out to Get the Mail, To Kiss the Worms Goodnight,* and *The Girls*. A fifth, *The Flower Lover*, followed in October. For each of these poems, Martin paid Bukowski $30—pretty good money for a man whose real job brought home about $100 dollars a week. For the first time in his life, Bukowski began to think he might actually be able to quit the workaday world and make it on his writing alone.

In the meantime, Martin completed his leap of faith by selling his entire collection of modern first editions to the University of California, Santa Barbara for fifty thousand dollars (about thirty of which was left after taxes and fees) and investing the whole kit and caboodle into Black Sparrow. He picked up a few more rising stars in poets Robert Duncan, Ron Loewinsohn, and Michael Forrest; the disparity between their styles and Bukowski's proved he had no more of an agenda than printing authors he liked to read.

Bukowski appreciated Martin's unshakeable faith in his own taste, and his detachment from the insular and incestuous literary scene that divided authors into "schools" and "movements" and made editors into spokesmen for the trends *du jour*. He also loved his new publisher's soft-spoken, no nonsense demeanor and business acumen. The pair could hardly have been more different from one another. Martin abstained from tobacco, gambling, drugs, and alcohol, and was a church-going man, devoted to his family. He dressed well, steered clear of the counterculture, and never engaged in the heated arguments Bukowski so loved to start. But after years of dealing with fellow madmen and emotionally unstable women, Bukowski was glad to find someone he could trust implicitly, someone who carried no baggage and reduced their personal interaction to its barest essential—Martin paid him to write. Excepting perhaps Buk's collaboration with Carl Weissner, this simple arrangement formed the basis of the longest running and least contentious relationship Bukowski ever had.

Limited edition broadsides and poems in small-circulation magazines were not going to make Bukowski famous, however. Until Black Sparrow was fully operational, he needed to find another outlet, something that would reach more eyes and minds and create a real following to buy the books John Martin was promising to print. He happened upon the perfect answer when John Bryan asked him to write a column for his new underground newspaper. Of course, it is only in retrospect that such a linear progression can be assigned to Bukowski's career. At the time, Bukowski viewed every opportunity to publish as a happy accident—good for sustaining morale, but not likely to lead to any major success, financial or otherwise. That was certainly the case with *Open City*, Bryan's new weekly; "they let me write anything I wish. might stop doing the damn things soon. poems first, or living first, hell yes," he wrote in 1967 (*Screams*, 213). It was Bryan's idea to call Bukowski's column "Notes of a Dirty Old Man"—the paper specialized in new music reviews and articles on the drug culture and perhaps he hoped Bukowski would help round out the formula for "Sex, Drugs, and Rock 'n' Roll"—but Bukowski was all too happy to fill that role. Editing interference was minimal to none. He had carte blanche to write about whatever he pleased and it must have been liberating to have another outlet beyond his letters to just let the words flow and not worry about their literary merit or confining himself to "the straight jacket of Art."

As in his letters, Bukowski's columns tended to ignore standard punctuation, capitalization or spelling. The style was colloquial, brash, and pure Bukowski. He did not bother to hide behind a pseudonym, and though he embellished quite a bit, most of his early articles were based on his own experiences: the fight with Robert Baume and bashing in the handyman's head with his portable typewriter, burying his father, his short-lived marriage to Barbara Frye, meeting Neal Cassady. In each of these stories, he managed to slip in just enough talk of sex or some other transgressive behavior to keep his readers titillated and coming back for more. As his store of autobiographical anecdotes began to dwindle, the weekly demand for more of the same kept him constantly in search of new material. He began to borrow from the lives of his friends and associates, often depicting them in an unflattering and inaccurate manner for greater effect. Nobody was safe from the "Dirty Old Man," no matter how much respect he had proclaimed for his subjects in the past; Jon Webb, Douglas Blazek, et al. were fair game and repeated targets. Needless to say, none of them appreciated the treatment and more than a few egos were badly bruised in the process.

The public ate it up, however, and Bukowski acquired quite a local following. *Open City*'s circulation was in the thousands, and, with issues coming out weekly, Bukowski was quickly exposed to more readers than he had reached through all of his past publications combined.

Black Sparrow published two more Bukowski broadsides in 1967. The first, simply titled *2 Poems*, contained the works "Family, Family" and the deceptively simple "A Little Atomic Bomb." In the latter, he trained his wry gaze on a subject that still had most of the world petrified and diffused its power by reducing the bomb to a bathtub plaything. The second broadside, *The Curtains Are Waving*, featured just the titular poem. Those who try to track down original copies of these early works will almost certainly find themselves stymied. Approximately a hundred of each was printed and the vast majority of those have disappeared into the remainder bin of history. Fortunately, those three poems were subsequently included in *The Days Run Away Like Wild Horses of the Hills*, *Play the Piano Drunk Like a Percussion Instrument Until the Fingers Bleed a Bit*, and *Burning in Water Drowning in Flame* (respectively).

In May of 1968, Black Sparrow capitalized on Bukowski's growing *Open City* readership by putting out *At Terror Street and Agony Way*. Not quite as large, nor as extravagantly produced as his two Loujon Press collections, it nonetheless became another instant collectible, thanks to some unintentional special features. The first regards its harrowing journey to publication. Apparently, Bukowski had brought his only copies of some poems over to John Thomas's house one night, with the idea of making a recording. The pair of them liked to stay up late popping speed, drinking beers, and shooting the breeze. Many nights Thomas recorded their conversations onto a reel-to-reel machine. He was interested in "heard poetry," the sound of natural speech, and was recording all kinds of things in those days. It just so happens that night it was Bukowski reading. The original manuscripts for those poems got misplaced, nobody seems to know what happened to them, and they were forgotten. Bukowski heard the tapes sometime later, identified the poems and the voice as his own, and when Martin came to him with the idea of putting out something larger than a broadside, Bukowski suggested he use the poems preserved on tape.

The curse attending these poems did not end with the lost manuscripts. Initially, eighteen copies of *At Terror Street and Agony Way* were printed with "Street" misspelled at "Sreet." 747 additional copies appeared with a white label glued on to correct the misprint. Martin also printed ninety hardcover copies; each was signed by Bukowski and contained an original drawing "tipped in" as a kind of frontispiece. Finally, fifty copies of the recordings themselves were sold to collectors at ten bucks a pop. In a shrewd bit of cross marketing, all three states of the book included an excerpt of Bukowski's August 20, 1967 letter to Michael Forrest "blind stamped" onto the last leaf of the book. Forrest was a fellow poet, and the second author that Black Sparrow published. In the excerpt, Bukowski is complaining melodramatically about work, depression, and the weather. Interestingly, the parts of the letter *not* excerpted contain much more valuable biographical information. In these, he admits to having a falling out with the Webbs over his account of a recent visit to their new home in Tucson (where they had moved for health reasons), written for his *Open City* column, which he assesses rather offhandedly: "I don't think it was a dirty column. only factual." (*Screams*, 312–313). Then he goes on to mention that he had recently applied for a grant from the Guggenheim Foundation. Evidently, Bukowski had been working on a novel since at least December 1966, tentatively titled *The Way the Dead Love* ("We" sometimes replaced the second "the"), and had submitted the work in progress with the idea of getting money to finish it. In another letter to Wantling, Bukowski downplayed both his hopes of winning the grant and his former association with John William Corrington, by saying he had only applied at all because "some prof who teaches at Loyola" had suggested it (*Screams*, 308). Clearly Bukowski was hedging his bets, emotionally and professionally. But as he predicted, the proposal was rejected and despite telling Jon Webb that the novel was "easy to write" and "a free day or so and I have 5 or 10 more chapters," Bukowski never finished it (*Screams*, 297). Without belaboring the point, it seems likely that not getting the Guggenheim played a large role in him abandoning the novel. Deep down, the opinion of the establishment still mattered to him.

The Guggenheim rejection aside, Bukowski had plenty of projects to keep him busy. In the summer of '68, Poetry X Change, a small press in Glendale, California put out another of his chapbooks called *Poems Written before Jumping out of An 8 Story Window*. In late '68, John Bryan landed him a deal with Essex House, a publisher of "adult reading," to collect his more memorable *Open City* columns into book form, earning him an impressive $1000 advance. For a paycheck that fat, Bukowski was willing to slum around with a less than reputable publisher. In the decade to come, whenever money was extremely tight, Bukowski continued this trend by turning out stories for the skin mags, catering to their kinky tastes with ribald tales full of juicy details. But there is a fine line between edgy literature and outright pornography and Bukowski did not always walk it successfully. When John Bryan asked him to edit a literary supplement for *Open City*, Bukowski selected "Skinny Dynamite," a controversial story by Jack Micheline about a young girl's sexual exploits that promptly got Bryan arrested on obscenity charges. The case was eventually dropped but *Open City* collapsed amid the resulting furor. As if helping to sink his friend's newspaper was not bad enough, Bukowski rubbed a little salt into the wound by subsequently writing a bitingly satirical short story called "The Birth, Life and Death of an Underground Newspaper" (later included in *Erections, Ejacuations, Exhibitions and General Tales of Ordinary Madness*). Once again, Bukowski could not resist the urge to burn a bridge once he had crossed it.

Fortunately, for Bukowski, his relationship with John Martin remained as rock solid as ever. Working with someone as efficient and business-like as Martin gave Bukowski a taste of how professional publishers could operate, and after a decade of dealing with often flaky little magazines and newspapers he began to crave more control and consistency, not to mention a chance to disseminate his own take on what constituted worthwhile literature. He never stopped nursing his dream to quit the post office (it is easy to forget he was still working full-time during this period) but to do that he would need another steady source of income. With the exception of his inclusion in the Penguin Modern Poets series, a coup that would not have been possible without the influence of Harold Norse, the mainstream publishers were still too conservative to go anywhere near him. So in early 1969, Bukowski channeled his disgust with both ends of the publishing spectrum into his own magazine.

His partner in this enterprise was Neeli Cherkovski, a young poet and son of friend Sam Cherry (nee Cherkovski). Neeli was somewhat of a Bukowski disciple in those days; he and Buk spent a lot of late nights drinking and arguing over literature, and

Cherkovski is said to have constantly carried around a notebook with him, to write down every *bon mot* that dribbled from Bukowski's drunken lips. Clearly, these notes must have stood him in good stead when he set about twenty years later to become his hero's first official biographer.

After some deliberation, they settled on one of Bukowski's trademark attention-grabbing titles, *Laugh Literary and Man the Humping Guns* (Bukowski wanted "Fucking" instead of "Humping" but better sense won out). As when he helped Barbara Frye edit *Harlequin,* Bukowski had difficulty keeping in check his resentment over slights real and imagined; he and Neeli were often merciless in their rejection letters, especially when the authors were people they did not like. They also clearly had an axe to grind with poets then in vogue and threw down the gauntlet with the following words printed boldly on the cover of issue number one: "In disgust with poetry Chicago, with the dull dumpling pattycake safe Creeleys, Olsons, Dickeys, Merwins, Nemerovs and Merediths."

Beyond provoking noted laureates and settling petty vendettas, Bukowski and Cherkovski were able to repay a few favors and promote the work of writers they respected. Among those included in the three issues of *Laugh Literary* published from 1969 to 1972 were Harold Norse, John Thomas, Douglas Blazek, Steve Richmond, Jack Micheline, and Jerome Rothenberg.

Bukowski's double life as a controversial writer and civil servant finally collided when someone at the Terminal Annex informed the bosses about his *Open City* gig and his child born out of wedlock. The post office authorities, in turn, informed the FBI. An investigator came around to interrogate the Crottys (his landlords) and a few neighbors about his political leanings and lifestyle. Then, one day Bukowski was called into the personnel office and confronted with several copies of the newspaper. The managers thought they had a smoking gun and obviously expected him to deny any involvement, to sweat their stern looks and threats of termination, but Bukowski played it cool and calmly admitted he was the author behind "Notes of a Dirty Old Man." He also reminded them of his First Amendment rights. Fearing a blowback even worse than the relatively minor scandal of a disreputable employee, the managers backed off and Bukowski walked out of there feeling he had bested the system for once in his life.

For many Americans, 1969 signaled much more than the last year of the decade. It was the death of a dream, the end of an era. The assassinations of Martin Luther King and Robert Kennedy in 1968 presaged a string of violent and disturbing acts the following year that collectively clouded the national horizon and rang a death knell on the flower power generation: Charles Manson and the Tate-Bianca murders, the ugly incident at Altamount, nationwide race riots, and nearly 10,000 Americans killed in Vietnam.

In that context, it is telling that 1969 was a banner year for Bukowski. His brand of grim realism, leavened here and there with gallows humor and picaresque flourishes, clearly spoke to disillusioned America, as evidenced by the extraordinary amount of Bukowski material printed and read that year. In addition to 28,000 copies of *Notes of Dirty Old Man*, the Penguin Modern Poets book, the first issue of *Laugh Literary*, an 80-page *Bukowski Sampler* (published by Doug Blazek), another broadside called *If We Take*, and the first ever critical study of Bukowski's work (Hugh Fox's *Charles Bukowski: A Critical and Bibliographical Study*) that year also saw the appearance of Bukowski's first truly full-length Black Sparrow collection. *The Days Run Away Like Wild Horses over the Hills* was published on December 30, in 1,243 copies. Like almost all of Black Sparrow's books, the jacket was a paragon of simplicity, bearing nothing more than title and the name of the author. Most of the poems inside were culled from the previous chapbooks and underground magazines and the specter of Jane haunts a good number of them.

Roughly concurrent with the release of *The Days Run Away Like Wild Horses over the Hills* were two other events that unequivocally mark 1969 as a major turning point for Bukowski. The first is the now legendary offer from John Martin to pay Bukowski $100 a month to quit his job at the post office and write full-time. This nice round figure was actually the result of the two men carefully tallying Bukowksi's monthly expenses. For Martin, who still had his own family to support and a business to run, it represented a substantial sum and a financial risk. For Bukowski, it was certainly a big leap of faith, just not quite as voluntary or as reckless as the legend would have us believe. Howard Sounes discovered that Bukowski's employment record tells a slightly different story. Apparently, a letter from his superiors was sent to Bukowski in the fall of '69, warning him that he was going to be fired for missing too many days, and suggesting he resign to avoid disgrace. Scrounging for a backup plan, Bukowski went to Martin and promised plenty of new material in return for the monthly stipend, failing to mention that he had no other option. Martin agreed and the rest is history (Sounes, 101).

The real story hints at another side to Bukowski that often gets left out of standard characterizations of him as a freewheeling gambler and spendthrift. The truth, according to those that knew him best, was that Bukowski was a frugal man who paid his bills on time, seldom lent money to friends, and only gambled with money he did not strictly need. At the time he left the post office, he had thousands in a savings account (some of it still socked away from his inheritance), and about the same in a pension fund. However much he hated his father, some of the old man had slipped into him. This helps explain why he stuck it out for so long at the Terminal Annex, despite the tediousness of the job and the terrible wear on his body. He simply could not bear to go back to the days when he survived on candy bars and beer. He also had Marina to think about, and the monthly child support payments. Understanding these pressures, and their effect on Bukowski, helps crystallize just how scary and exhilarating it must have been to sever that lifeline and set out to survive on his writing ability alone.

There is some discrepancy over when, exactly, Bukowski was liberated. Taking his cue from Buk's mid-November letter to Carl Weiner, Seamus Cooney (editor of the three-volume set of Bukowski's *Selected Letters*) suggests that Buk tendered his resignation "[a]t the end of November 1969" (*Screams*, 353). Sounes, usually more exact, puts the date sometime in December (Sounes, 103). Neeli Cherkovski situates that fateful day early in the new year, confidently stating that "on January 2, 1970 Hank quit his job at the post office." (Cherkovski, 223). These may seem like minor quibbles, but establishing the order of events might help us to better zero in on Bukowski's state of mind at the time. Whenever it actually happened, the result was the same. As Bukowski put it in a letter written January 11, 1970:

> I am a member of the unemployed now with nothing but a typer and a couple of paint brushes to hold off the world. So keep your fingers crossed for me and hope the gods are on my side.
>
> (*Screams*, 354)

A good indication of his income concerns, and the second pivotal event in 1969, was that Bukowski finally agreed to give a public reading. It took place at The Bridge, a bookstore/gallery on Sunset Boulevard owned by Peter Edler, as part of a poetry series featuring Harold Norse, John Thomas and other local poets. Previous nights had attracted a few dozen attendees, but Bukowski's inaugural reading drew hundreds. Everyone agrees that Bukowski read brilliantly—so brilliantly that he was invited back for an encore performance the following night that was equally well attended and received—but recollections of the date of the reading also differ somewhat. Cherkovski, who was there, remembers it happening in the "spring of 1969" (Cherkovski, 211), well before Bukowski quit the post office. Sounes, drawing on numerous interviews as well as a February 1970 review of the reading by John Thomas, pegs the date more precisely as December 19, 1969, just before Buk escaped the Terminal Annex. Both cite the opportunity to bring in a little extra cash as the primary motivating factor, so again the point is essentially moot, but Sounes's version sure makes for a dramatic climax to Bukowski's most successful year to date.

# CHAPTER FIVE

# Ordinary Madness

*I think you'll like Post Office, maybe even better
than Notes. There's plenty of sex in there for laughs
and enough horror and madness to float the type-
script to you across the Atlantic. I try to photograph
rather than preach.*

—Charles Bukowski, *Living on Luck,*

IT SHOULD BE CLEAR by this point that Bukowski was a difficult
man to pin down. And not just chronologically. Was he a lazy
bum who lay about all day drinking beer in his underwear? Yes,
but was he also a disciplined writer with a hefty dose of German
fortitude and an ear for classical music? Yes indeed. Did he gamble
and drink away money better spent on more practical things? You
bet. Was he also a thrifty man who made a dollar last longer than
most. Yep, that too. Did he covet the respect and admiration of his
peers? Yes, albeit secretly and selectively. Did he also despise literary criticism and any form of academic writing? With a passion.
Was he an ugly ogre with a cruel heart and a mile-wide streak of
vindictiveness? Sometimes. Did he adore his daughter with a ten-
derness that would shame Mr. Rogers? No question. Take the
following excerpt of a letter included with his child support pay-
ment in September 1969:

Sometimes when I get sick I think about you and it makes me well again. PLEASE BE VERY CAREFUL WHEN YOU CROSS ANY STREET. LOOK *BOTH* WAYS. I think about you all the time and love you more than the sky or the mountains or the ocean or anybody or anything. Please stay well and happy and don't worry about me.

(*Living on Luck*, 89)

Given all this vacillation between extremes it is no surprise that the first few weeks of 1970 saw him caroming from drunken depression and laying sick in bed to manically churning out pages at a clip to rival Kerouac's legendary speed with *On the Road.* He wrote his first novel, *Post Office,* in about three weeks, working on it ten hours a day and revising as he went along. Twelve straight years of toil and frustration poured out of him in simple, clipped sentences. He stuck pretty close to the facts, relating how he got started at the post office (kicking things off with the now trademark phrase, "It began as a mistake"), what the job entailed, how mean his supervisor was, living with his "shackjob" Betty (the character based on Jane), and the hazards of dogs, bad weather, and lonely housewives.

It was all fairly pedestrian stuff, but the unique voice with which he delivered it inspired interest, camaraderie, and most of all laughs. A barrel full of laughs. Henry Chinaski was a regular guy, the kind we all knew. He was just trying to get by, working one of the million meaningless jobs that make the world go round. He was a wise-ass and a screw-up, always horny or hung over or both—in short, the kind of man who refused to be romanticized. He was not fighting for some greater cause, or the love of a good woman, or even his own soul. He just wanted what we all want—a life without too much hardship, a few creature comforts, a warm bed, and somebody to share it with.

When he completed *Post Office,* Bukowski turned again to poetry for a while and continued producing at an amazing rate. Letters to Weisner and Cherkovski in the spring of 1970 indicate that somewhere between thirty five and fifty new poems—"as good or better than any I have written" Bukowski breathlessly reports—were written within a period of several weeks. (*Living on Luck*, 95) What's more, he had also begun a new novel, which he was then calling *The Horseplayer* (later to become *Factotum*).

Signs that he was achieving at least some degree of literary importance began to manifest themselves. John Martin arranged to have UC Santa Barbara buy an assortment of Bukowski's personal papers for five thousand dollars and Sounes reports that, in April of 1970, a collection of Bukowski first editions was auctioned off by an unnamed individual in New York, "alongside collections of Faulkner and Hemingway" (Sounes, 106). In May he was invited to read at the University of New Mexico and Bellevue Community College, in Seattle, the latter necessitating his first ever plane ride. Both events were big hits despite the advanced state of inebriation required to get Bukowski up on stage.

Bukowski turned fifty in August of that year and was keenly aware of the great unknown he was entering, at an age when most men were looking forward to retirement. Despite all the outward indications of promise, he was still plagued by self-doubt. Carl Weissner was busy translating *Notes of a Dirty Old Man*, John Martin was readying *Post Office* for publication, but Bukowski never stopped worrying about his income, or lack thereof. To fill the gaps in his budget, he wrote stories for porn mags like *Fling*, lacing them with sex scenes that were outlandish even by his standards. A second attempt at securing grant money, this time from the National Endowment for the Arts, resulted again in failure.

In times like these, Bukowski needed companionship to keep his mind from eating itself. Not the kind of unsatisfying company afforded by visiting sycophants, or even the comfort of a good friend. No, he needed a woman. Someone he could spar with, sexually and emotionally. Someone to recharge his aging batteries and get his blood running again. For better or worse, that is exactly what he found.

Linda King clearly had the most raw sexuality of all Bukowski's lovers. She was also the most unbalanced. Twenty years his junior, King was one of the many high-spirited and headstrong women of the period who waged their own liberation movement, not by marching on Washington or organizing bra-burning protests, but by directly confronting and provoking the men in her life. King's freedom came with a price, however. Not only was she another casualty of a failed marriage, like Jane Cooney Baker and FrancEyE before her, she had also suffered a nervous breakdown and spent time in a mental institution receiving electro-shock therapy.

After moving to Burbank with her two children, King dabbled in several bohemian pursuits, from acting, to writing poetry, to sculpting. She lacked talent in the first, was still developing her abilities in the second, but showed a lot of promise in the third and "the sculptress" is how Bukowski most often referred to her (when he wasn't using less flattering epithets).

King first caught sight of Bukowski at a poetry reading at The Bridge, sometime in late 1970. She had met Peter Edler there and, in discussing the local scene, Edler had mentioned Bukowski. His name spoken, the devil duly put in an appearance later that night, but he did not stay long enough to meet her (the only poetry readings Bukowski could stomach were his own, and even those often brought on bouts of actual vomiting). A few weeks later, Edler brought King around to Buk's place on De Longpre, and she kicked off a flirtatious evening with an attention-grabbing rendition of one of her own poems. What she lacked in eloquence she apparently made up in flare. Bukowski was in the middle of another sexual dry spell, and immediately set about trying to seduce her. For her part, King looked at Bukowski more as a personal challenge than a possible lover, at least in the beginning; she had notions of taming his chauvinism. Nevertheless, a switch was thrown that night and the current ran through both of them.

Linda toyed with Hank for a while, enjoying the power his attraction gave her. To spice up the courtship, she sent him a poem in which she called him a troll and dared him to "come and frolic / with the liberated Billies" (Sounes, 112). With the poem was a letter and in the letter was an offer to sculpt his bust. King knew full well neither his ego nor his libido would permit him to refuse.

The flirtation continued in King's kitchen while the bust took shape. Dozens of letters were sent back and forth. Bukowski talked about old lovers while King challenged him with her progressive ideas, then aroused him with dirty talk, warning him that any man who wanted to be with her had to master the fine art of cunnilingus. Old Buk knew nothing about it. King would fix that before long.

Eventually the sexual tension became too strong to withstand any longer, and the two went to bed together, but Bukowski's Valium habit at the time, when combined with his prodigious beer intake, made it difficult for him to perform. King helped him lose some weight and clean out his system and a few weeks later the relationship was finally consummated. Bukowski quickly became infatuated with the younger woman, a dangerous state for someone so prone to jealous rages. King was vivacious and gregarious at parties; she liked to dance and flirt playfully with other writers and artists. Bukowski would watch her all night, simmering with rage. Sometimes he contained the inevitable explosion until later, when they were alone. Sometimes he did not. The volatility of their relationship and the frequency of their public meltdowns contributed to the growing Bukowski legend. People showed up at parties where they knew he would be just to see what might happen.

King's bust of Bukowski was not only an excellent likeness, but also became a symbolic totem as well—its whereabouts providing an accurate indicator of the state of their relationship. If it was at Bukowski's place, all was well (relatively speaking); if it had been returned to Linda (or unceremoniously wedged in her screen door, etc.), then their friends knew the affair was on the skids. Eventually, bronze replicas of the bust were made and sold to collectors, but the run was abbreviated and extant copies are quite scarce indeed.

*Post Office* was published in midst of all this, on February 8, 1971. It is not quite clear why it took a year from the time Bukowski finished it to when it was released to the public. Perhaps, after the deluge in 1969, Martin wanted to avoid flooding the market with even more Bukowski material, but at least part of the delay was editorial. Cherkovski reports that "editing decisions regarding *Post Office* were not monumental" and that the only changes Martin suggested were "simply typesetting details" but once again Bukowski's correspondence helps to recover the truth.

(Cherkovski, 226) A letter to Martin on May 10, 1970 reveals that the publisher was thinking of including a glossary with the novel, presumably to explain some of the postal terminology Bukowski uses. "I can't agree with you on the dictionary idea for the novel," Bukowski says, "but if you insist, we'll go ahead.... I think though that most of the terms are obvious, even to an outsider ... [and] the dictionary has a cheapening and commercial effect.... Think it over a while." (*Living on Luck*, 98) Two more letters to Carl Weissner, who was already at work translating *Post Office* for release in Germany, suggest additional disagreements. "Martin has me worried," Bukowski confides, "I'd prefer *Post Office* in its original raw form." (*Living on Luck,* 106) He goes on to explain that the major sticking point was his use of mixed tenses. "I know most of the rules of grammar but I'm not interested.... He's a nice guy but he does treat me too much like an idiot. He admits I'm his best seller but at the same time he'd rather I wrote more safe shit." The second letter (August 8, 1970) reveals Martin's fear that the Germans would beat him to the punch and release the novel first. Weissner had already published his edition of *Notes of a Dirty Old Man* and though it only managed to sell about twelve hundred copies, despite the invention of a Henry Miller plug for the book jacket, Weissner was eager to put out something else (Sounes, 109-110 and *Living on Luck*, 93).

Assessments of Martin's editorial involvement throughout his collaboration with Bukowski typically run to one of two extremes. Many assert that Martin was either completely hands off or that Bukowski refused every change ever suggested. Others claim Martin actively attempted to sanitize Bukowski and go so far as to describe the publisher as some sort of Svengali who, out of jealousy or some predatory business instinct, helped orchestrate the destruction of Bukowski's other partnerships. In a review of *Mockingbird Wish Me Luck* (the 1972 poetry collection containing the piece "300 Poems" that slighted Steve Richmond) posted to Amazon.com, an anonymous "reader" with a writing style similar enough to Richmond's to leave little doubt about the reviewer's identity unleashes a tirade that reads in part: "Publisher Martin has to rejoice at this collection which grants Martin his first scorpian [sic] like inroads into the grisel [sic] of a super strong amer-ican poet of us people AND BY NOTHING MORE COMPLICATED THAN INSECT POISON PUSHES BUKOWSKI TOWARD THE FINAL KAHLIL GIBRAN KIND OF WEAK SPIRITUAL LOVE GROPING OF SLIMEY SLOBBER POESY BUK ENDS UP WRITING HIS LAST DAYS AROUND THESE PARTS.... Martin hides behind Bukowski's levis by publishing Buk poems which grossly lie about various literary artists MARTIN RESENTS." As ridiculous as it might be to quote from an online book review (for another laugh, see Richmond's review of his own book, *Spinning Off Bukowski,* on the same site), if nothing else it shows how much emotion Bukowski's words can incite almost thirty years after the fact.

Regardless of the editorial route *Post Office* took on its way to publication, the reading public greeted it eagerly on arrival. The first run of two thousand sold out almost immediately, and it has gone on to sell upwards of fifty thousand copies.

The success of *Post Office* caught the attention of another enter-prising small publisher, Lawrence Ferlinghetti. Beat poet and founder of City Lights bookstore, Ferlinghetti was already familiar with Bukowski—the two began corresponding in 1969—but whatever ambivalence he felt about Buk's poetry was rendered moot when he realized just how popular Buk was. The two of them were soon discussing the idea of assembling a collection of Bukowski's short stories.

While that partnership was forming, another was permanently terminated. Ailing and estranged from his favorite writer ever since Bukowski wrote that slanderous article about him for *Open City,* Jon Webb died in June 1971, signaling the end of one of the most distinctive small presses in American publishing.

Bukowski's feelings toward Linda continued to boomerang from obsessive love to green-eyed fury. She called him on faults few had thrown in his face before, characterizing his constant angst as a distorted form of narcissism and his drinking a cowardly screen against reality. When she went back to Utah to visit family, as she did every summer, Bukowski nearly went mad without her, firing off a flurry of panicked phone calls and lovestruck letters.

King placated him as best she could, promising her fidelity, but was increasingly chafed by his possessive attempts to leash her natural independence.

More fights erupted in public and private when King returned. On at least three occasions, the police were summoned to help calm things down. One night after a particularly contentious party, when the witnesses had all gone home, Bukowski broke King's nose with a sudden blow to the face. For a brief time afterward, it looked like King might have reached her limit. She tried to break away, and succeeded for a time, but soon they were together again. Something on Bukowski's hook kept reeling her back. She even moved into an apartment behind Bukowski's and collaborated with him on a chapbook called *Me and Your Sometimes Love Poems*, published in 1972. It would be several more years and multiple breakups and reunions before they severed their relationship for good.

In the summer of '72, during one of their cooling off periods, King returned to Utah and Bukowski began an affair with a woman named Liza Williams. An acquaintance from the late '60s, when they both wrote columns for *Open City*, Liza was older than Linda and less fiery, but still attractive enough to catch Bukowski's eye. She was also quite successful and well connected in the music industry. When they got together, she was president of Island Records, the label responsible for, among other things, introducing Bob Marley and other reggae artists to the States. As such, Williams was in a position to pamper Bukowski. She treated him to a week-long vacation to Catalina, an island off the Southern California coast, and several other getaways up the coast. She also let him stay at her fancy pad in the Hollywood Hills, where she hosted many exclusive parties, and introduced him to the hip musicians and artists who attended. Bukowski had little use for the vast majority of these people, whom he considered vapid and untalented, and he spent most of his time coldly eyeing the crowd, but a few slipped past his defenses and became friends—colorful characters like R. Crumb, the hugely popular underground comic book artist who would later illustrate several of Bukowski's books. Another was the young film director Taylor Hackford, who went on to direct *An*

*Officer and a Gentleman* and *The Devil's Advocate*, among other Hollywood blockbusters. The two of them apparently hit it off so well that Hackford was soon accompanying Bukowski on his daily trips to the racetracks and drinking with him well into the night. Then working in public television, Hackford began to formulate plans for making a documentary on his new friend. Bukowski liked the idea, and gave Hackford the green light.

Between his tempestuous reunions with King and cushy rendezvous with Liza Williams, Bukowski also managed to find time to court through the post a twenty-seven year-old airline stewardess and fan of his writing named Patricia Connell. Bukowski wrote her a spate of at least eleven letters in three months (August–October, 1972), in which he downplayed his love triangle with King and Williams while slyly suggesting they make it a quadrilateral (in another letter to Weissner, Bukowksi hints at a fourth woman, waiting in the wings and even younger still). Bukowski's constant updates on his love life would be downright comical if one could not so easily imagine the tectonic upheavals that accompanied them. On September 13, he writes, "I broke off with Liza and went back to the sculptress (Linda)." On September 18, "ah, I am back with Liza." Four days later, he writes, "you won't believe it—I'm back with Linda." (*Living on Luck*, 162-164) Needless to say, both women were emotional wrecks, but Liza bore the better share of the hurt, as she was not accustomed to Bukowski's games. For her part, King continued to play along with consummate skill, breaking into his place one night while he was with Williams and stealing back her bust. In the end, Liza never really had a chance—again and again in his letters, Bukowski admits that he never really loved her the way he loved Linda. By early '73, King had edged Williams out of the picture for good and even convinced Bukowski to move into her new house in Silver Lake, but their battles were far from over. As Bukowski succinctly put it in a letter to Carl Weissner, "There's no rest, there's no victory, there's no meaning, and love comes in salt-grain size." (*Living on Luck*, 166)

Lest someone get the wrong idea, Bukowski accomplished much more in 1972 than rubbing elbows and tying love tangles. If anything, his writing output increased. In addition to continued work on his second novel, Bukowski edited and published *An Anthology of L.A. Poets* with Neeli Cherkovski and Paul Vangelisti, collaborated with Linda King on the aforementioned chapbook, wrote more stories for the *L.A. Free Press* (which had picked up his column after the demise of *Open City*), and churned out enough new poems for John Martin to release another collection, called *Mockingbird Wish Me Luck*. A January letter to Carl Weissner also mentions several translations in the works.

However, it was City Lights who made the biggest impact on Bukowski's career in 1972. After nearly a year of editing and preparation, Ferlinghetti released *Erections, Ejaculations, Exhibitions and General Tales of Ordinary Madness*. Split eleven years later into two volumes called *Tales of Ordinary Madness* and *The Most Beautiful Woman in Town*, *Erections* ran to nearly five hundred pages and contained many of the best short stories Bukowski ever wrote. Thanks in part to Ferlinghetti's imprimatur, the book did particularly well in Northern California, paving the way for a City Lights-sponsored reading in September at the Poets Theater. Taylor Hackford accompanied Bukowski north and shot footage of the event for his documentary. His stock was not wasted. A capacity crowd turned out—800 tickets sold out in advance, a fact that particularly pleased Bukowski as Ferlinghetti had promised him half of the evening's take—and Bukowski gave one of his most memorable performances ever. He was stone drunk, as usual, and stricken with terrible stage fright, but none of that showed when got on the mic and riled the crowd with his commanding and combative presence. As much proto-punk happening as literary event, the rowdy reading was followed by an even more raucous party at Ferlinghetti's apartment, where a select cadre of San Francisco's countercultural literati gathered to get royally soused with the man of the hour. Bukowski met and exceeded their expectations. He had reconciled with Linda King for the weekend, but old jealousies flared almost immediately and, as Sounes relates in his lively prologue, their reunion devolved into a violent spat that scattered the guests, shattered windows and door panels, and ultimately summoned the police. Despite the destruction, Ferlinghetti delivered on his promise and handed over $400 the following morning (Sounes, 5). As much as he hated the pressure and the circus atmosphere surrounding his readings, Bukowski was forced to concede their earning potential. He would give many more over the course of his career, most of them equally successful, and in the years to come he would raise his fee to $1000, plus travel expenses, partly out of the hope that such a figure could not be met, thereby releasing him from an obligation to read. But demand for his readings was high and he almost always got what he asked. A decade after Jon and Gypsy Lou Webb voted him "Outsider of the Year," dark horse Bukowski was making a move for the inside track.

For a little while, Bukowski's life with Linda at the house in Silver Lake was inordinately calm and domestic. Contact with his daughter Marina had been sporadic over the years since his split with FrancEyE, especially when FrancEyE took her to live in a New Mexico commune, but now that they were back in Santa Monica and with Linda's two children providing perfect play-mates, Bukowski was able to have Marina come and stay with him on the weekends. He also began to attend some of her school functions, and generally play a larger role in her life. Despite its irregularity, the father-daughter bond between them remained extraordinarily strong. The letter cited at the beginning of this chapter makes it clear that, in some ways (beyond standard advice on the crossing the street), Marina played the parental role in their relationship by providing Bukowski with his one unconditional and unadulterated source of comfort and happiness. In return, Marina seemed to ask very little of him; she must have intuitively understood he was a different kind of father and simply enjoyed spending time in his company. As Sounes and other interviewers have reported, Marina's memories of her childhood were not unhappy ones. On the contrary, she remembers always feeling loved and well cared for by her father, who had a talent for com-municating on a level she could understand. Both their special connection and this curious form of role reversal are captured beautifully in the short story "A .45 to Pay the Rent" (from *Erections ...*), in which a stick-up artist and his daughter play-act as "baby" and "mama" while shopping in a supermarket. Another touching testament is Bukowski's *Love Poem to Marina* (reprinted here courtesy of Black sparrow Press), which Black Sparrow published in a limited-edition broadside in 1973:

my girl is 8
and that's old enough to know
better or worse or
anything
so I relax around her and
hear various astounding things
about sex
life in general and life in particular;
mostly, it's very
easy
except I became a father when most men
become grandfathers, I am a very late starter
in everything.
and I stretch on the grass and sand
and she rips dandelions up
and places them in my hair
while I doze in the sea breeze.

I awaken
shake
say, "what the hell?"
and flowers fall over my eyes and over my nose
and over my
lips.
I brush them away
And she sits above me
giggling.

daughter,
right or wrong,
I do love you,
it's only that sometimes I act as if

you weren't there,
but there have been fights with women
notes left on dressers
factory jobs
flat tires in Compton at 3 a.m.
all those things that keep people from
knowing each other and
worse than
that.

thanks for the
flowers.

Bukowski found additional pleasure in his by-now automatic routines of writing a bit each day and going to the racetracks. Work on *Factotum* continued (albeit in fits and starts), the poems seldom stopped writing themselves for more than a few days at a time, and Carl Wiessner was busy translating the stories from *Erections ...* into German.

Inevitably, the roof caved on this semi-blissful home life. Letters to a young woman named Joanna Bull reveal continued infidelities, but even without outside interference Hank and Linda's relationship was always a few too many drinks away from implosion. The fights in public and the bouts of drunken madness began all over again. On at least one occasion, Bukowski went berserk and started tearing up the house. The cops came and took him away, but according to Sounes they turned out to be big fans of his work and let him off with nary a slap on the wrist. In the summer of 1973, King invited Bukowski to join her on the annual return to Utah. Extended hijinks ensued when Bukowski, an inveterate city dweller, got lost in the backcountry. Five years later the public would get to share in Bukowski's torment by reading a hilarious account of the ordeal in his third novel, *Women*. Back in LA, the star-crossed lovers picked up right where they left off. Linda caught Bukowski visiting one of his girlfriends one day and nearly ran him over with her car. Miraculously, their relationship survived these and many other attacks on each other's mental and physical well being and, though Bukowski moved out of King's place at the end of July, their love affair limped on for another two years.

In the middle of October, Bukowski and an auditorium full of friends and fans were treated to an early screening of Taylor Hackford's documentary. In addition to priceless footage from the Poets Theater reading, the film featured intimate and gritty scenes from his daily life, hiding none of his faults and allowing him ample opportunity to extemporize about his life. Once again, Bukowski was faced with a double-edged situation in which ego-gratification came shaken and stirred with ample snorts of embarrassment and exposure. While the film was received warmly that night, and would go on to win an award for "Best Cultural Program" from the Corporation for Public Broadcasting (despite drawing the public's ire for its liberal inclusion of obscenities), many of Bukowski's friends from his "Outsider" days responded to his newfound fame with bitterness and derision. Part of this was fueled by John Martin's refusal to publish them and Bukowski's unwillingness to step in on their behalf. Part of it was simple jealousy. By the end of 1973, Black Sparrow had put out their own collection of Bukowski's short stories (*South of No North*, comprised mostly of pieces left out of *Erections ...*), City Lights had paid him a ten thousand dollar advance for their reprint of *Notes of a Dirty Old Man*, his readings were better-attended and received than most rock shows, and the National Endowment for the Arts had recently rewarded his long-standing requests with a five thousand dollar grant.

However, Bukowski certainly did not endear himself with his continued boorishness and insensitive behavior. One of his more despicable habits was hitting on women (in print and in actuality) whose lovers or husbands had recently passed away. The first example of this was his father's fiancé, whom he more or less rapes in a *Notes of a Dirty Old Man* piece while another man beats his wife in the other room (Bukowski is careful to include an earlier scene in which the woman comes on to him). Who can say what actually happened, but the imagining of it can at least be partially explained by his extreme hatred for this father. That justification cannot be used for the story he wrote for the *Free Press* about Jon Webb's death, in which he tries to bed a poorly disguised Gypsy

Lou after the funeral in the crudest manner imaginable. But even that betrayal pales in comparison to the Shakespearean backstabbing of his former friend William Wantling.

In the spring of 1974, Wantling asked Bukowski to give a reading at the college in Illinois where he was teaching at the time. They had continued to correspond, and their work appeared in many of the same publications, but they had yet to meet face to face. Like numerous other warm and respectful long-distance relationships that turned sour in person, it would have been much better for both of them if they had kept their distance. Bukowski had long chided Wantling for his decision to "go academic" and seldom failed to make his opinions known. Interviews that Sounes conducted with Wantling's widow, Ruth, suggest Bukowski delivered a substandard reading to an audience unappreciative of his alcohol-fueled shenanigans, and then ruined the reception afterward by regaling those in attendance with surly silence. Until that night, Wantling held Bukowski in the highest regard and was crushed when his idol came toppling down from his pedestal. This disillusionment contributed to Wantling's pre-existing psychological instability and, together with his rampant heroin addiction and failing marriage, sent him on a downward spiral. A few weeks later, Bukowski pulled his standard trick of converting his experiences into barbed columns for the *LA Free Press* and wrote two scathing pieces on Wantling (lazily pseudonymed "Howard Stantling") that depicted him as washed-out and pathetic. No one can say for sure whether Wantling read the pieces, but shortly after their appearance he drank himself to death.

Sounes's interviews with A.D. Winans (a mutual friend of Bukowski and Wantling) and Steve Richmond indicate that Bukowski felt a degree of guilt over his contribution to Wantling's demise (particularly for his harsh rejection of some poems Wantling had submitted to *Laugh Literary and Man the Humping Guns*), but evidently not enough to keep him from repeatedly propositioning Ruth Wantling when she visited Los Angeles shortly after her husband's death (Sounes, 137). When she refused, Bukowski viciously attributed her husband's self-destruction to some kind of sexual frigidity on her part. He also included a description of the episode in *Women*, his third novel, written several years later. As he remarked in a July 25, 1974 letter to Carl Weissner, "Down in a motel in Laguna one night I snarled at [Wantling's] x-wife (death is divorce, isn't it?), 'No wonder the son of a bitch had to take the needle for 9 years. He was living with you." (*Living on Luck*, 193). At least he did not feign surprise when Ruth demanded his foreword be stricken from Wantling's posthumously published poetry collection, *7 on Style*.

While Bukowski's stateside friendships and alliances continued to disintegrate and develop with equal frequency, Carl Weissner remained as loyal as ever, quietly and tirelessly promoting his client and expanding his readership abroad. Cherkovski and Sounes differ somewhat on the exact order in which the German translations were published, but both agree that the minor impact made by the German edition of *Notes of a Dirty Old Man* became a major groundswell when Weissner and Benno Käsmyr, a young editor/publisher, decided to put out a collection of Bukowski's verse in German. Lifting the title from his 1968 chapbook, *Poems Written Before Jumping Out of an 8 Story Window*, Weissner and Käsmyr convinced a large chain to stock it and the book just took off, ultimately selling fifty thousand copies. Subsequent collections of short stories (Weissner wisely selected the best from *Erections ...* and spread them out over three volumes) sold somewhere in the neighborhood of eighty thousand apiece, and a compendium of excerpts from *Post Office* and *Factotum* and more short stories (alternately titled *Stories and Novels* or *The Blue Book*) sold nearly a hundred thousand. In 1922, Bukowski's father had left Germany in search of greater riches in America. His son must have enjoyed the irony in his reversal of that trend over fifty years later.

As if cinematic plaudits and international bestsellers were not enough to keep Bukowski's spirits afloat, Black Sparrow capped off 1974 with the milestone publication of *Burning in Water Drowning in Flame*. A retrospective of his poetic output to date, the book was divided into four sections comprised of poems selected from his two Loujon Press books, his first Black Sparrow collection (*At Terror Street and Agony Way*) and a final section showcasing new poems written from 1972–73. In the twenty odd years since he had begun writing poetry in earnest, Bukowski had produced 8 full-length collections (albeit with some overlap of material), at least three times that many chapbooks and broadsides, and individual poems in the thousands. In the twenty years left to him, he would continue to produce at a rate unsurpassed by any other American poet. As Russell Harrison astutely points out in *Against the American Dream*, Bukowski was more prolific than every other major poet now being studied in the universities. Of course, the question of quality must be considered with that of quantity; nonetheless, Bukowski's massive oeuvre becomes even more conspicuous when seen in the light of its almost complete ostracizing by academia. If nothing else, it is worth studying how an inveterate misanthrope did more to democratize poetry than any other American writer, living or dead, without having any kind of design or agenda. Dockworkers, bartenders, housewives, cabdrivers, and hookers all read his books, and often it was the only thing they read. And this is perhaps where Harrison falters, in associating Bukowski's work ethic with overblown and out-of-context notions of "the proletariat." For Bukowski, it was simply about his own struggle with the word, a battle waged not with brief salvos of inspiration or brilliant strokes of strategy, and certainly not for any overthrow of capitalism. No, Bukowski hunkered in the trenches, night after night, year after year, decade after decade, pounding the keys and putting in the work, because he could not live any other way and his readers empathized with that. Sure, a lot of what he wrote was not worth the typewriter ribbon used to create it. But editing was for editors and analysis for the critics. Bukowski was a *writer*, nothing more and nothing less—one whose readers appreciated his humanity, his willingness to bear his flaws and his weakness, and still swing for the fences. Perhaps he himself put in best in a letter to Weissner written just one month after the publication of *Burning in Water Drowning in Flame*. While most poets would have paused and basked in the glory of a watershed moment, Bukowski went right back to work, grinding out the words. "Have written a hundred and ten poems in the last two weeks," he writes, "a few of them are shit; 7 or 8 of them are immortal." (*Living on Luck*, 194).

# CHAPTER SIX

# Homecomings

*There aren't many women I know of who've met*
*Bukowski and* didn't *fall in love with him. I know*
*this because many of them have told me so. And I*
*think the main reason they did was because of his*
*beat-up, fearless, bestial face, the kind of face that*
*looks good to a lot of women, like it did to the fairy*
*tale Belle, and makes them feel, when juxtaposed to*
*that archetypal, gritty gruffness, smooth, intuitive,*
*and eternally beautiful.*

—Joan Jobe Smith, *Das ist Alles:*
*Charles Bukowski: Recollected*

ANOTHER SPLIT WITH LINDA KING in July of 1974 afforded
Bukowski more time to devote to his four favorite activities:
writing, drinking, betting on the horses, and womanizing. Work
on *Factotum* slowed down a bit during the fall while he maintained a fairly rigorous (and profitable) schedule of readings
around the country, pumped out pieces for the *LA Free Press*, and
continued sparring with the poem. He had presciently kept his
bungalow on Carlton Way during his cohabitation with Linda,
and most of his neighbors there were fellow lushes and carousers,
so loneliness was not a problem. He enjoyed spending time with

one couple in particular, named Brad and Tina Darby. Brad managed both the apartment complex and a nearby sex parlor, while Tina danced at one of the clubs downtown. The three of them went to a lot of parties together and burnt the midnight oil on Carlton Way. Perhaps the most evocative record of Bukowski's life during this period is a little volume called *The Buk Book*, put out by a small press in Toronto, not so much for the capsule biography provided by critic and author Jim Christy (though it does contain some racy, otherwise unpublished anecdotes), but thanks to two series of photos by Claude Powell that accompany it. Powell was a young friend from Bukowski's days on De Longpre Ave. and knew the Darbys as well. The first set of photos, dated from 1971, shows Bukowski clowning around in soiled boxers, cigar in hand, hair unwashed, looking like the last man on earth a woman would desire. Three years later, Powell took a second set with a recently purchased Polaroid camera. As Jim Christy tells it, when the Polaroids developed, Tina Darby felt Bukowski looked too sad in them, presumably over the breakup with King, and proceeded to cheer him up by slowly shedding her clothes and letting Powell take pictures of them in lewd poses. The resultant shots capture the myth of the Dirty Old Man even better than anything he has written—a bearded, crater-faced ogre grinning and leering impishly at the lithe and willing nude girl in his lap. But the story of the Powell's Polaroids also has an epilogue. The following day, more friends were over and the naughty photographs inevitably came out for everyone's enjoyment. Linda King chose that moment to arrive unannounced. And all hell broke loose when she saw the Polaroids. Snatching them from the hands of whoever held them at the time, King managed to rip up a few before Bukowski lunged at her and landed atop his coffee table, smashing it to pieces. King and Tina Darby then scuffled, with King pulling on Darby's broken and splinted pinky finger until the poor girl screamed for mercy. Darby ran to her place and retrieved a .38 revolver, but fortunately King had left by the time she returned. At least partial corroboration of the whole sordid affair can be found in the pictures themselves, as reproduced in *The Buk Book*, for the most suggestive of them bear evidence of tearing and repair with scotch tape.

Another infamous photo of Bukowski from this period segues nicely into his next affair. In it, Bukowski is standing in the kitchen of his place on Carlton Way, longish hair brushed back over his brow, beard graying prematurely around the edges, pale belly pushing out between his belt and the hem of a too-small t-shirt, his arm around the waist of a woman who would be not unfairly be described as a homely tart. Both of them have beers and cigarettes in their hands, as if to chase a quickie assignation (there even seem to be dusty fingerprints on the woman's skirt), and both have their eyes at half-mast, but while the woman looks addled, Bukowski's face hides a wily intelligence. I know what *you* think of her, the smug smirk on his face seems to say, but *I* don't give a damn.

The woman in the picture is named Georgia Peckham-Krellner and despite all appearances, she is not the other woman in the affair that finally cleaved the tragic bond between Bukowski and Linda King. That honor belongs to her friend, Pamela Miller, a.k.a. Cupcakes. Peckham-Krellner was a fan of Bukowski's writing and it was on the occasion of her thirtieth birthday that Cupcakes first contacted her friend's literary hero. The pair was out celebrating at a bar and round about last call Miller rang up Bukowski and asked if the two of them could come over and meet him. As Sounes explains, Bukowski kept his number listed for just such an occasion; he even wrote a poem about it (Sounes, 151). Bukowski liked the sound of Miller's voice and said a visit was fine by him. When the women arrived Bukowski saw that Miller's body was every bit as appealing as her voice. A strawberry blond with big breasts, pretty eyes, and a B-movie-star face, Miller had everything that Peckham-Krellner did not. She even preferred to go by the pet name of Cupcakes. Apparently, the one thing she lacked (and Peckham-Krellner had in spades) was an agreeable personality. Again, as Sounes tells it, Bukowski said as much that first evening, suggesting he could make an ideal woman by merging the two of them together. Returning to the photo, one can almost read Bukowski's affection for Peckham-Krellner on his face; he seems to be testing the viewer, challenging us to look beyond their disheveled, unattractive appearance and find the salt-of-the-earth human beings that lived beneath. And if we cannot, well then, we are not worth his concern anyway. (For those wishing to view the photo in question, an Internet search should result in success. Alternately a hard copy can be found in the second signature of photos in the Sounes book.)

Bukowski had never let a character flaw get in the way of his libido before, and he was not about to start with Cupcakes. Peckham-Krellner may have been the nicer of the two, but Cupcakes had a figure straight out of his adolescent fantasies. And everything else about her fit the profile as well; knocked up at fifteen, now a single mom, she was half his age, loved to party, and thrived on the attention her looks garnered her. The year before she had even been crowned Miss Pussycat Theaters by the chain of x-rated movie houses she worked for. But, like Linda King, she was prone to fickle moods and flirting, and she drove Bukowski crazy by cutting contact with him for days at a time time. She also played very hard to get.

Meanwhile, Linda King discovered she was pregnant. She had recently been with other men (mostly to spite Bukowski) so she could not be certain who the father was, and because of that she could not count on Bukowski for support, and clearly a stable home life was out of the question. King decided to get out of Los Angeles and move to Arizona. Sadly, the exertion of readying the house for sale sent her into premature labor and she lost the baby to miscarriage. Grieving and still recovering from her hemorrhage, she called Bukowski to tell him the bad news, but apparently he did not empathize very much and crassly informed her, with evident glee, that Cupcakes had consented to sleep with him at last, on the condition that he replace his soiled mattress. The new bedding duly delivered, Cupcakes was at that very moment out buying a celebratory bottle of champagne.

The next night Linda was drinking wine and nursing her wounds when the thought of Bukowski's insensitivity raised enough ire to send her over to his house in search of revenge. He was not home when she arrived (Sounes has him at the racetrack, Cherkovski out of town giving a reading) so she broke in and rounded up everything he might truly miss—his typewriter, radio, some drawings, paintings, first editions of his books—and either destroyed them outright or piled them into her Volkswagen.

When Bukowski returned from wherever he was, he found King hiding in his bushes, hysterically angry and nearly unhinged. The old lovers squared off and had one last knock-down, drag-out row. Bukowski, tried to talk sense to King, begging her to spare his books, but instead she started hurling them through his windows like errant baseballs. Then she set about demolishing his typewriter by smashing it repeatedly against the pavement. Bukowski was forced to call the cops and watch them haul her off to jail. No charges were filed, however, and King moved to Arizona shortly thereafter.

Amazingly enough that was not quite the end of their relationship. Some months later, Bukowski flew out to Phoenix for a visit. Though they slept together and toyed with the idea of reuniting, both of them knew it was a hopeless cause. Bukowski flew back to Los Angeles alone and never laid eyes on King again.

Bukowski finally finished his second novel, *Factotum*, sometime in 1975; it was published in December of that year. The title, a word from Medieval Latin meaning a servant or employee who is assigned all manner of chores (essentially "jack of all trades" but without any positive connotations), came straight out of the dictionary one day when he was searching for a term to capture his itinerant lifestyle in the forties and all the odd jobs he took to stay alive. Sifting his memory of those years for a coherent narrative must have been nearly as difficult as living through them in the first please (the writing took about half as long, almost four years), but the result was far superior to his first effort in almost every respect. Whereas *Post Office* has the feel of a one-off monologue by a likeable raconteur, *Factotum*'s broader historical context and more controlled tone takes that solipsism and somehow inverts it to include the entire working class—a subtext that is exhaustively explored by Russell Harrison in *Against the American Dream*. Sounes cites George Orwell's *Down and Out in Paris and London* as the book's primary inspiration, but Gay Brewer convincingly points out the book's similarities to Bukowski's old favorites, Knut Hamsun's *Hunger* and John Fante's

*Ask the Dust* (Brewer, 18–21). Undoubtedly, *Factotum* was influenced by all three, together with Bukowski's own unique experience, but where it differs (and perhaps surpasses them) is in its edgy intermingling of nihilism and humor, somehow maintaining a revolutionary stance against capitalism without taking itself very seriously or to resorting to political polemic. Bukowski certainly felt proud of it when he was done, writing to Carl Weissner, "I'm hot on *Factotum*, my last novel. Ya seen it yet? I think it's the best writing I've done. Have gotten quite a bit of mail about it agreeing with me" (*Living on Luck*, 214).

Like always, he did not sit on that smug satisfaction for very long. A letter to John Martin written a little over a month after the publication of *Factotum* indicates he was already thinking about a third novel about his various affairs, or as he called it in another letter, "the MAN-WOMAN situation" (*Living on Luck*, 203). Bukowski's working title at the time, *Love Tales of the Hyena*, gives some forewarning about the tone and the shape he expected his next novel to take.

Semi-serious boasts about fan mail aside, Bukowski was keenly intent on retaining his humility, regardless of how successful he got. This noble goal would become increasingly more difficult to meet in the years ahead, as his fame outgrew literary and local contexts and entered the vastly larger arena of pop culture. Taylor Hackford's documentary for public television may have begun that process (a February 1975 screening of it at the Whitney Museum in New York, and subsequent write-up in the *New York Times*, evidently boosted his renown significantly), but the first true sign of the nationwide cult of Bukowski came in October of 1975, when *Rolling Stone* magazine decided to write a feature on him. A letter written at the time to fellow poet Charles Plymell is worth quoting at length, as it makes no bones about Bukowski's reaction to such attention from the mainstream media and shows just how savvy he really was.

> The whole problem is how serious a man can take what the media does to and/or for him. What one should realize is that the media puffs up a hell of a lot of stale fruitcake ... Most creative artists are

weak because they are emotional, and because it's hard and dirty work even though it's most interesting work. They fall to exposure, camera flashes, that grisly attention. I think that when any creative artist gets good enough society has an Animal out There that the artist is fed to so he won't get any stronger. Creativity, no matter what you say, is somehow bound up with adversity, and when you get dangerous enough they simply take away your adversity. They've done it with the blacks, they've done it with the Chicanos, they've done it with the women, and now they're playing with me. I intend to allow them to clutch a loud, empty fart for their reward. I will be elsewhere, cleaning my toenails or reading the *Racing Form.*

(*Living on Luck,* 206)

John Martin must have expressed some worry that all this exposure would distract Bukowski from his writing. It was seven months before the *Rolling Stone* article actually appeared and when it did, Bukowski had this to say about it: "that's just another test the mother gods are laying upon me. I ain't going to wilt to the sound of late trumpets semi-heralding a late and minor fame. Please don't worry about me, boss, I am too crazy to go crazy" (*Living on Luck,* 219). As if to prove Bukowski's point, the *Rolling Stone* article perpetuated an apocryphal assertion that Jean Paul Sartre and Jean Genet were great fans of his writing. Howard Sounes made an effort to verify the origins of this idea with leading experts on both French authors and arrived at the conclusion that it was completely fabricated (Sounes, 142).

Both a significantly more viable threat than fame to Bukowski's sanity and a nearly foolproof insurance against the unchecked growth of his ego emanated from the women in his life, particularly Cupcakes Miller. Rebounding from his dramatic break with Linda King, Bukowski fell desperately hard for the younger woman and though she thrived on flattery and attention, and though Bukowski often gave her money to buy her daughter new dresses and the speed to which she was hopelessly addicted, Miller had little to no appreciation for poetry or Bukowski's literary renown. Unlike Linda King, she had no abiding respect for his creative force and so the connection between them was much more tenuous, at least from Cupcakes' perspective. (When asked nearly twenty-five years later to make a contribution to *Drinking with Bukowski*, a collection of reminiscences and tributes, she could barely summon the motivation to write what looks to be a two-paragraph email message. Although she has kind words about Hank and fond memories of their relationship, sullied somewhat by bitterness over the treatment she later received in print, her overall assessment of their love affair is not one of much depth or weight.)

A temporary split with Cupcakes in March of 1976 allowed Bukowski the opportunity to explore other relationships, in addition to the seemingly endless succession of one-night (or possibly one-hour) stands he had with woman who showed up on his doorstep eager to test the legend of the Dirty Old Man. A letter to John Martin mentions two women in Texas—"Katherine" and "Suzanna"—in terms that suggest some degree of emotional involvement. But sometime in the spring of 1976, Cupcakes came back into the picture when she moved into his apartment complex on Carlton Way. Having such an inveterate *femme fatale* in such close proximity had a disastrous effect on Bukowski, especially when she pulled one of her disappearing acts. A series of notes he wrote to her while ignorant of her whereabouts, included in *Living on Luck*, reads like the diary of a man on the edge of a manic breakdown. Bukowski admits as much in an uncharacteristically terse letter to John Martin on May 3: "I have gone a bit mad, and there's a reason" (*Living on Luck*, 218). Fortunately, he retained enough sense to know he had to get away from her and clear his head. Various readings around the country sometimes provided him the opportunity, but at other times she accompanied him and further crazed him with her behavior. On at least one occasion, he actually read love poems to her while she was sitting in the audience but she was too high to properly appreciate the gesture.

Throughout the summer and early fall Cupcakes continued to jerk Bukowski around and dominate his thoughts to the extent that his writing on his third novel slowed to a standstill. He received more national exposure, though of a decidedly different sort, via an interview in *Hustler* magazine, Larry Flynt's more risqué answer to Hugh Hefner's *Playboy*. The magazine had recently purchased a couple of his stories and Bukowski must have enjoyed being flown out to Columbus, Ohio (Flynt's hometown and headquarters) and briefly immersing himself in a milieu where his chauvinism could run rampant, but a letter to Carl Weissner suggests he got an even greater thrill from knowing it was the birthplace of James Thurber, his favorite satirist and an author who, like Bukowski, had a penchant for augmenting his writings with playful illustrations.

Bukowski's affair with Cupcakes reached an all-time low in September when the voluptuous redhead turned to prostitution for some extra cash. Evidently it was not exactly a new thing for her—Bukowski refers to her in a September 13 letter as "the former part-time hooker"—and she felt no compunction about Bukowski knowing it. On the contrary, she asked him to cash one of her client's checks for her! (*Living on Luck*, 222) The same letter contains a very telling admission of longing on Bukowski's part, made all the more poignant by subsequent events.

> I am luckier than most; I have various other sources of fulfill-ment—female, of course. But I doubt that there is any real woman upon the horizon (for me, my mind, my need, my weakness) and I'll probably go to my death without ever seeing her—which hardly makes my life any different from another man's. Yet I keep feeling that she's out there, somewhere, but how do you get to her?
>
> (*Living on Luck*, 222)

Not only would Bukowski find this "real woman" a short two weeks later, but doing so required little more of him than attending one of his own readings.

It happened at the Troubadour, a Santa Monica club where Bukowski gave one of his last stateside appearances. The woman was Linda Lee Beighle, a petite blond who had been coming to his readings for over a year, and enjoying his poetry for considerably longer, without ever introducing herself. That night might have been no different—Bukowski brought Cupcakes along and had she not gotten wasted and left early, her bombshell looks and obstinate personality very well could have scared off the much more reserved Beighle—but as Bukowski left the club with a friend, she seized her chance and approached him. After some typical fan-to-author small talk, they exchanged phone numbers and left it at that.

On the one hand, Linda Lee shared many traits with other women in Bukowski's life. Like Barbara Frye, she came from a wealthy family that had smothered her individuality and instilled an early itch to break out on her own. Like Linda King, she ran away fairly young and ended up in Southern California. Like FrancEyE she nurtured a deep spirituality and an interest in progressive ideas, manifested most outwardly in her devotion to an Indian guru named Meher Baba and her commitment to a healthy diet. Like Cupcakes, she refused to immediately hop into bed with Bukowski, although for quite different reasons (Meher Baba forbade sex out of wedlock). And like nearly every woman with whom Bukowski ever associated, Linda Lee enjoyed drinking and could apparently keep up with him well into the evening.

But unlike all the others, she does not seem to have been drawn to Bukowski out of some deep-seated, neurotic need for attention, conquest, validation, or masochistic abuse. She was not a groupie, a vamp, or an addict. She had no real artistic ambitions (beyond a few acting classes) that might benefit from a brush with a famous poet; she was self-sufficient, financially and emotionally; and she had neither an ex-husband nor any children to look after. In short, she was probably the most level-headed, mature, and baggage-free woman that Bukowski ever met.

At first, these traits failed to cement much of a connection between them, at least from Bukowski's perspective. The ban on sex was enough in and of itself to keep him seeing other women. He also had trouble relating to her New Age tendencies. When they met, Beighle owned a health-food restaurant in Redondo Beach called the Dewdrop Inn, where hippies congregated and tried to convince each other that the sixties represented more than a flash in the brainpan of American consciousness. On Bukowski's first visit there, several days after their meeting, he found little with which he had in common and felt entirely out of place. Besides, all manner of women were still writing, calling, and paying Bukowski visits and even if his third novel had not provided a perfect excuse to study (read: bed) as many as humanly possible, he simply lacked the moral fiber or the motive to turn them away. He was still operating under the notion that he had to make up for all the time he spent alone and horny as a young man. And, after all, he had a reputation to maintain.

Gradually, however, Linda Lee's quiet strength and persistence won out. Bukowski was chafed by her possessiveness but, in his advancing age, greatly appreciated her sincere concern for his health. It must have occurred to him that, at the rate he was going, it would not be long before he would need a caretaker and though one hates to characterize his change of heart as a matter of convenience and practicality, it would probably not be too far from the truth. After all the unhealthy and destructive relationships he had been through in the past, one can hardly fault him for finally choosing nurturing, if tepid, tranquility over passionate turmoil.

Hugely instrumental in this maturation process was the opportunity to flush all the other women out of his system, both literally and figuratively. Cupcakes ducked out of his life entirely one day with hardly a look back. As mentioned earlier, one final fling with Linda King in Arizona amounted to nothing, and all the others were mere trifles—belt notches in one of the more acute mid-life crises in the annals of American malehood.

By the fall of 1977, Bukowski had finished his third novel, now simply called *Women,* and written enough good new poetry for John Martin to put out another collection. *Love is a Dog from Hell* appeared first, and functions as a good companion piece to the novel (published almost a year later), in that the subject matter is the same and both afford the more nosy of his fans their best opportunity to match pseudonyms and descriptions with real people and ferret out the juicy details of Bukowski's love life. Once again, Bukowski was elated by his accomplishment. Letters to Martin contain his standard proclamations: "*Women* is my proudest and best work," and "I await *Women* unlike I've ever awaited any other book. As I wrote it I could feel it happening—that certain carving into the page with certain words in a way that you feel the power and the magic and the luck" (*Living on Luck*, 248–249).

Sometime in 1977 or early '78, Bukowski received a call from a French director named Barbet Schroeder, who expressed keen interest in developing a film with him. Never a fan of the medium, and all too aware of the degradation the business had inflicted on writers he respected like Faulkner and Fante, Bukowski was indisposed to the idea (his first reaction, as quoted in several sources, was "Fuck off you French frog!") but Schroeder made a convincing pitch, emphasizing his sincere appreciation for Bukowski's work and his desire to do it justice. After Bukowski got over his distaste for Schroeder's accent, he realized what a lively character he was. Born in Iran while his German geologist father was on assignment, raised in France and South America, he attended the Sorbonne in Paris and worked variously as a film critic, jazz concert promoter, and news photographer before founding his own production company. Bukowski's good impression of him was heightened when the two met face to face, drank away an evening at Bukowski's place, and Schroeder showed him some of his work. Primarily a director of documentaries up to that point, Schroeder had done compelling films on Koko, the first gorilla taught to communicate with sign language and another on the Ugandan dictator Idi Amin. On the surface, such subject matter might have alienated Bukowski (what writer would want to be associated with a sadistic politician and a talking gorilla?), but he recognized the passion with which Schroeder approached his material and his talent for capturing the kind of subtlety and nuance that too often eluded Hollywood. Ultimately, the door was left open on the idea of collaboration and a new friendship was begun.

It was not the first time Bukowski had received an offer to adapt his fiction to film. Taylor Hackford had purchased the rights to *Post Office* around the time his documentary was made, but so far nothing had come of it. Taking the next step with Schroeder would require additional meetings before Bukowski could fully trust the man to represent his work faithfully.

By early 1978, Bukowski was avowedly monogamous and planning a trip to Germany with Linda Lee. He had been thinking about visiting Carl Weissner and his Uncle Heinrich for years, but perhaps lacked the nerve before he had Linda by his side to look after him. They flew out of L.A. on May 9 accompanied by the German-born photographer and friend Michael Montfort, with the idea of publishing an illustrated travelogue when they returned (what later became *Shakespeare Never Did This*). True to form, Bukowski got blotto on the trip over and seldom sobered up during their three-week stay. Beyond resulting in a chronologically confused account of his trip, this nearly constant state of inebriation, combined with Buk's anxiety about his homecoming, occasionally made for some wild encounters, starting with the customs authorities in Frankfurt who were a bit too zealous for Bukowski's taste. Linda was keen on visiting all the major sites but Bukowski apparently had little patience for castles and quaint shops. Nevertheless, they spent over a week traveling about by train and doing the tourist thing before setting off for Hamburg, where Bukowski was scheduled to give his one reading of the trip. Even given the popularity of his books, everyone was surprised by what a huge crowd he drew, especially as it was on short notice. People came from as far away as Holland and Austria for the chance to see their hero in person. The German novelist Gunter Grass had read in the same venue, an old market building on the waterfront called The Markhalle, several months before and not attracted anywhere near as many.

Despite his standard case of the jitters, Bukowski gave another command performance. He had worried that the language barrier would prove problematic, but if anything the Germans were even more attentive to the actual words read than their American counterparts.

Next up was the long-awaited reunion with Uncle Heinrich in Andernach. By all accounts a spry and feisty man of ninety, fluent in English, Heinrich Fett was ecstatic to see his nephew, despite being woken from a nap when Hank and Linda arrived. Bukowski worried about imposing on the old man, so after a joyous visit in his home, he and Linda begged their leave and returned to their hotel but soon enough Uncle Heinrich showed up, raring to go again. He showed Hank and Linda around town, pointing out the building on Aktienstrasse where Bukowski was born (and revealing its recent history as a brothel, a fact that must have pleased Bukowski to no end).

The trip also gave Bukowski the chance to spend some quality time with Carl Weissner and his wife and son. Buk was immensely grateful for what his translator had done for him and, moreover, genuinely adored the man with an enthusiasm that never waned throughout all the years they knew each other.

There were also, of course, numerous interviews with the German press and several nights out drinking with the Weissners, Montfort, and a handful of friends and hangers-on. The night following Bukowski's reunion with Uncle Heinrich was especially emotional. He is said to have consumed seven bottles of wine all by himself and regaled all those in attendance with tales of his past.

A snafu in their itinerary forced them to fly out of Paris, where they again met with Barbet Schroeder for another pleasant evening of good wine, food, and conversation. Bukowski's account of the visit in *Shakespeare Never Did This* reveals his great affection and growing respect for the director, a mutual admiration that would see them through the years of effort and tribulation that it took to see their plans come to fruition.

Back home in the States, Bukowski faced a predicament wholly unprecedented in his experience. By the late '70s, royalties from the sale of his books (both stateside and abroad) were so extravagant that he risked owing an outrageous amount to the IRS if he did not invest in some property. This rude shock instigated an intensive review of his business dealings, particularly with John Martin. Bukowski's monthly stipend had long ago been raised to a figure more in keeping with the current cost of living and the amount of revenue his Black Sparrow books actually generated, but Bukowski still suspected he was owed more and especially resented Martin taking a cut from his foreign sales. The heated atmosphere cooled off a bit after a complete disclosure revealed that Martin was more or less current on his payments, at least as far as his contractual obligations went, and despite Linda Lee and others pressuring Bukowski to find a new publisher, he remained loyal to his old friend.

In the midst of all these financial headaches, Bukowski was somehow convinced to return to Paris when a French talk show named *Apostrophe* offered to fly him and Linda over for a taping. Quite popular in France at the time, *Apostrophe* was a round-table affair hosted by an effete arbiter of taste named Bernard Pivot that gathered leading artists and intellectuals and gently probed aesthetic issues of the day. As might be expected, Bukowski was not thrilled by the idea of another stressful trip but knew it would help foreign sales; he felt pressure from his French publishers, and fancied another visit with Carl Weissner. His translator was not a wealthy man and a train to France was much more feasible than a flight to the U.S.

Bukowski's demands for his appearance were the same he made for his readings—alcohol must be provided (by this time he had graduated to drinking mostly wine, and not the cheap stuff either) and all expenses must be paid. Knowing what an exclusive they would be getting, especially in Europe, the producers of the show readily agreed.

His account of the second trip abroad is included in *Shakespeare Never Did This* and though it inaccurately precedes the section on Germany, it contains a vivid description of the affair. The French must have had some idea what would happen if they threw the ornery and scandalous American into a ring with stuffy European intellectuals (in this case a head shrink known primarily for psychoanalyzing the avant-garde playwright Antonin Artaud and a female author with whom Bukowski was unfamiliar) but even so they were completely unprepared for what unfolded. Bukowski loosened up in his usual manner beforehand and was thoroughly primed by showtime. He made it clear from the outset that he could not care less about the supposed honor it was to be there, disrupting the civilized atmosphere with a request to see more of the female guest's legs. Pivot tried to censor a string of obscenities by covering Bukowski's mouth, but only succeeded in bringing the American guest to his feet, whereupon he jerked out his translator earpiece and staggered off the set. There, he was confronted by a security guard and things nearly devolved to violence (and certain jail time) when Bukowski whipped out a small knife to ward away the guard, but Linda Lee somehow defused the situation and the two of them made a quick getaway.

It is impossible to know how much Bukowski staged of this episode (stills of the footage, included in Jean-François Duval's *Bukowski and the Beats*, show Bukowski wearing a maniacal jester's grin just before he stormed out) but whatever the case, his outrageous faux pas had an electric effect on French viewers. Wherever he went following the affair, he encountered people from all walks of life who applauded his snubbing of the snobs. Even the press was almost universally favorable. French translations of his books flew off the shelves. He was, after all, in the world capital of regicide and revolution.

Meanwhile, there was still the matter of finding a house stateside. After scouting several possible locations with Linda, they settled on a place in San Pedro, a harbor town at the southern tip of what can still be called Los Angeles. While the house was set back from the road, behind an ample hedge, and the unassuming suburban neighborhood provided Bukowski with a much needed modicum of privacy, it also was not too far from the freeway, allowing (as Cherkovski notes) a straight shoot to the racetracks at Santa Anita and Hollywood Park.

Bukowski and Linda moved into their new house in November 1978. Letters to Martin and Weissner written at the time reveal a growing impatience with the delay in the publication of *Women*, as well as continued frustration over bookkeeping hassles, but on the whole Bukowski seems to have settled fairly quickly into his new environs. He took up gardening and set about finding more tax loopholes by writing off his trips to Europe.

*Women* finally came out in the middle of December and promptly sent certain ladies' noses out of joint all over America, with its poorly disguised but amply detailed descriptions of his amours, most of which were either outrageously exaggerated or wholly false, according to the females in question. In Bukowski's defense, he does not exempt himself from the brutal deprecations and mirthful slander he inflicts on others. As both Howard Sounes and Gay Brewer point out in their books, Bukowski's alter-ego Henry Chinaski hardly gets a flattering portrayal, and neither do any of the other men in the book. Everyone is sacrificed at the altar of humor and ribaldry, and this is the likely reason why the book remains a favorite among readers of both sexes.

A letter to Gerald Locklin written just after the book came out helps explain its slow road to print and reveals continued tensions between Bukowski and Martin over editorial decisions. Nevertheless, Bukowski remained uncharacteristically subdued about the whole thing, once again giving Martin a length of slack denied to everyone else:

> On *Women*, a little tragedy there. Prefer you keep it fairly quiet. Like you know, I tell John Martin to go ahead and correct my grammar but this time he went too far. I should have read the proofs more carefully but am lazy.... Shit, man. I guess he thinks I can't write. He threw shit in. Like I like to say, "he said," "she said." That's enough for me. But he threw stuff in, like "he retorted," "he said cheerfully,".... Shit it goes on and on.... think of playing with Faulkner like that? Anyhow, I climbed him pretty hard for it and so the 2nd edition will read on a back page somewhere: "second edition, revised."
>
> (*Living on Luck*, 260)

Another unintended but happy result of the book's publication was that Bukowski got to meet and repay John Fante for all the inspiration he had provided him. Chinaski's citing of Fante and *Ask the Dust* prompted Martin to finally track down the writer (up to that point Fante was still so obscure that Martin thought Bukowski had made up the name and the novel). Loving what he read, Martin agreed to reprint *Ask the Dust* and Bukowski wrote a glowing and heartfelt preface. By that time, Fante was withering away in a Hollywood hospital, washed out of the movie industry and blind and legless due to a losing battle with diabetes. A meeting with Bukowski was arranged, and though Fante's infirmity made things a bit awkward, both men immediately recognized their kinship and developed a mutual respect. Fante was even inspired enough by the renewed interest in his work to dictate one last novel to his wife before succumbing to complications related to his illness in 1983.

Bukowski capped off this string of successes and personal milestones (and further evaded the covetously long arm of Uncle Sam) by trading in his beat-up old Volkswagen for a brand new car. Sticking with the Germans, he opted for a sleek black BMW. He had been driving around clunkers his entire life and took a perverse pleasure in bucking his image and buying the car outright. On the cusp of turning 60, the skid row genius was now comfortably middle class.

# CHAPTER SEVEN

# Curtain Calls

*Think upon this, O Los Angeles! At last you have a
resident culture hero who is neither actor nor freak!
Why, he could merge with any group of great men
and no one would be the wiser, no one could point
him out as the Gentleman from California ...*

    —John Thomas, *Bukowski in the Bathtub*

FOR A MAN WHO HAD spent his entire adult life seldom living
more than a few miles from Tinseltown, having zero interest in the
movie business, it is somewhat ironic that Bukowski's move to the
outskirts of the city coincided with a flurry of interest in adapting
his works to the silver screen. In addition to the ongoing project
with Barbet Schroeder, financiers in Italy offered over forty thousand dollars for the rights to adapt some of the stories in *Erections,
Ejaculations, Exhibitions and General Tales of Ordinary Madness*
(eventually producing the film *Tales of Ordinary Madness*).
Another group expressed interest in *Factotum* and, as mentioned
earlier, Taylor Hackford still held the rights to *Post Office*.

At Schroeder's prompting, Bukowski began work on his own
screenplay very early in 1979. Having had little exposure to the
movies, he found the new format confining at first, but his ear for
dialogue and trademark blend of humor and pathos came in very

handy. Bukowski chose to write about his time living in Philadelphia, hanging out in that memorable bar at 16th and Fairmount and stumbling into back-alley fights with bartender Frank McGilligan, but he changed the setting to L.A., compressed the timing of events, modeled characters on Jane Cooney Baker and Barbara Frye, and generally conflated various aspects of that part of his life into a more dramatically cohesive whole. Originally titled *The Rats of Thirst* (one can hardly imagine a title less suited to Hollywood), the screenplay was finished in April and eventually became known as *Barfly*. The ensuing wheelings and dealings behind the scenes, as Schroeder tried to secure financing and interest studios in the script, were ridiculously Byzantine, even by the infamous standards of that back-scratching industry. Because Bukowski so vividly and humorously captures them in his fifth novel, *Hollywood,* an attempt to do them adequate justice here would be futile. Interested readers, in particular aspiring screenwriters and directors, are heartily recommended to pick up a copy of his account and hear the stories firsthand. Suffice it to say that it took another eight years for the film to be made, and things got so bad that at one point Schroeder resorted to threatening self-mutilation with a circular saw while standing in front of a producer, in order to wrest back control of the picture and extract financial promises.

But the snafus did not end with the film's backers. After several rounds of considerations that included Kris Kristofferson, James Woods, and Tom Waits, a young Sean Penn offered to play the lead after he got a copy of the script. Already an avid Bukowski fan, Penn felt Dennis Hopper would be the perfect director for the material and agreed to do the film for the nominal fee of one dollar if Hopper got the nod. Penn, Hopper, Bukowski, and Schroeder met to try and hash out the details, but Bukowski was so turned off by the newly clean-and-sober Hopper and Schroeder so intent on maintaining control of the project (he turned down their offer of a producer's credit and a fat paycheck) that the talks fell through, and then Penn was out of the picture. Nevertheless, he and Bukowski remained very close friends and spent a great deal of time together over the next decade, with Penn becoming a

kind of surrogate son to Bukowski, never copping a superior atti-
tude as his fame ballooned. On several occasions, he even brought
along Madonna, his not exactly blushing new bride, but Bukowski
and the Material Girl were horribly incompatible and never
warmed up to each other.

While all this was happening, Bukowski somehow maintained
his usual schedule of writing, playing the horses, and managing his
literary affairs. Following the June 1979 publication of *Play the
Piano Like a Percussion Instrument Until the Fingers Begin to Bleed
a Bit* (his latest volume of verse), the completion of *Shakespeare
Never Did This* (his lively if muddled account of his European
adventures), and a trip to Vancouver to give another reading,
Bukowski began work on his fourth novel. Conforming to the pattern established by the first three, in which the subject matter
vacillated from recent events to those long removed (*Post Office*
being written just after he quit, followed by *Factotum's* recounting
of the earlier years, followed in turn by *Women*, the still-smol-
dering aftermath of his scorched-earth raid on the opposite sex),
Bukowski decided he was finally ready to tackle his youth and
early adulthood. Work on *Ham on Rye* began sometime in mid-
1980 and was finished about a year later.

Gay Brewer notes that, as with *Factotum*, the time between the
events chronicled and the writing of *Ham on Rye* made for greater
objectivity and a tighter structure (Brewer, 34). The interesting
result is that although it is his most strictly autobiographical novel,
Henry Chinaski becomes less of a pseudonym and more of a character study. Various aspects of his personality and outlook are not
only explored, but given context and psychological weight. Russell
Harrison also lauds the novel's "serious and extended [treatment]
... of issues that remained unexamined in the earlier novels: relations with and between his parents, relations to the social world of
his peers, and ... politics" (Harrison, 162). Bukowski clearly felt
compelled to dissect and explain some of his earlier actions and
motivations, including his alignment with Fascism, and was now
at an age and state of mind where he felt capable. The novel also
gave him the opportunity to plumb his obsession with class dis-
tinctions and avowed allegiance to the disenfranchised. Yet while

*Ham on Rye* finds Bukowski at his most self-reflective, it stops short of a full confession, ultimately revealing Bukowski as a man perpetually trapped between social longing and misanthropy, sovereign pride and self-loathing.

While stuck in financing limbo with *Barfly*, Barbet Schroeder took advantage of all the time spent in Bukowski's company and relieved his itch to pay tribute by filming his own documentary. Given a very limited release (excerpts were shown on French television), *The Charles Bukowski Tapes* are four hours worth of priceless footage, broken into fifty-two compact episodes. Each captures one thought or quote about Bukowski's life, and the vast majority involve little more than close-ups of the author addressing the camera, wine or bidi cigarette in hand, though Bukowski does give a mini-tour of L.A. and sites of personal importance, including the "house of horrors, the house of agony" at 2122 Longwood Ave, where the most infamous episodes from his childhood occurred.

Later that year, Bukowski and Linda Lee attended the U.S. premier of *Tales of Ordinary Madness*, the film cobbled together by Italian director Marco Ferreri from several Bukowski stories, and starring Ben Gazarra, a slick-looking fellow not at all right for the role. Bukowski came to the screening with low expectations and some lingering bitterness over the length of time it had taken the Italians to actually pay him monies promised in the contract, and the film did nothing to improve his opinion of the whole business. What it lacked in substance it tried to make up in shock value and failed on all accounts. Bukowski was left heckling his own image on the screen.

It was around this time that Bukowski's smooth ride with Linda Lee hit a patch of rough road. The trouble mostly derived from the generation gap between them and Linda's unwillingness to completely settle down and conform to his schedule and ever-shrinking list of preferred social activities. A huge fan of The Who (and personal friend of Pete Townsend), and other popular rock groups, Linda often went to concerts and other outings without Bukowski, maintained friendships with people her own age, and continued to follow the teachings of Meher Baba. That Bukowski resented her independence and the late hours she sometimes kept is made painfully obvious in one oft-mentioned episode from *The Charles Bukowski Tapes*, when Bukowski becomes suddenly enraged by her denials of such behavior, viciously kicks her several times—hard enough to knock her off the couch—and then calls her a "cunt" and a "whore." Though Linda later laughed at the violent outburst, characterizing it as an isolated aberration, the scene is ugly enough to make one wonder what other abuses she suffered offscreen. From 1981 to 1984, the couple fought often and Linda moved out at least three times, the third of which lasted the better part of 1983.

Bukowski's muse never left him, though, and his typer continued to clack, inexorably pumping out words like some internal organ. A new volume of poems (*Dangling in the Tournefortia*), a fourth novel (*Ham on Rye*), and another collection of stories (*Hot Water Music*) appeared in '81, '82, and '83, respectively. The latter found him at the top of his game and is often cited as his best work of short fiction. Leaner, cleaner, and more controlled than his past stories, many are told in third person and concern themselves less with the alienated artist waging private war against the world (where present, such characters are treated ironically) and more with capturing the complex dynamics of relationships in frank and subtle ways. Bukowski also teamed up with his old pal R. Crumb to produce illustrated editions of two short stories, *Bring Me Your Love* (1983) and *There's No Business* (1984). City Lights took a page out of Carl Weissner's book and split their unwieldy collection of Bukowski stories into two volumes, *The Most Beautiful Woman in Town and Other Stories* and *Tales of Ordinary Madness*, both of which became strong sellers in their own right. By 1984, Bukowski had also delivered enough new poetry for yet another collection, *War All the Time*.

All these publications, and the dozens that preceded them, began to bring in big bucks for Bukowski—$100,000 per year is the figure most often cited, and Howard Sounes confirmed this number with data from the IRS (Sounes, 280). Bukowski clearly resented being dubbed a "very rich writer" (and the implicit shift in focus from the writing to the writer) and asserted in private that the press exaggerated his income. "Where these boys get such fig-ures ... I don't know.... People are always pointing things out about me: I'm a drunk or I'm rich or I'm something else. How about the writing? Does it work or doesn't it?" (Bukowski, *Reach for the Sun*, 43).

Linda and Hank reconciled sometime in late 1984. Proof that he deeply cared about her welfare can be seen in his decision to cut her into his will for first a third and then half of everything for-merly slated for Marina alone (Sounes, 205). Then, in the summer of 1985, Bukowski surprised Linda with a proposal. As usual, there are two stories as to how this came about: one is that they were on the skids again and Linda reacted hysterically by going on a hunger strike. Fearful for her health, Bukowski offered his hand to appease her. The other version, as promulgated by a privately printed, extremely limited-edition Black Sparrow book called *The Wedding*, has Bukowski proposing to Linda rather suddenly in their garden, sans the emotional blackmail. Linda heartily accepted, but the ceremony was nearly cancelled (anything less would have been entirely out of character) when, just prior to the appointed day (August 18, 1985), Linda was stricken with the flu. With guests coming in from all over, Bukowski went into a panic that only became more acute when the doctor informed him that Linda needed serious medical attention. Yet, somehow, she rallied at the last moment and they went through with it. John Martin acted as best man and the wedding was held at the Church of the People, in Los Feliz. It was a small ceremony, attended by the Mar-tins, Marina and her boyfriend (later husband) Jeffrey Stone, Linda Lee's mother and sister, Michael Montfort and his wife, and maybe a half dozen others. Much larger was the reception fol-lowing, held at Siam West, a Thai restaurant in San Pedro, where a reggae band played and Bukowski got suitably hammered with old friends Steve Richmond and Gerald Locklin. The party spilled over into Bukowski's house in San Pedro and, by all reports, remained surprisingly civilized.

Like his brushes with fame, married life changed Bukowski very little. Part of every day was still devoted to writing and going to the track. Both journalist Paul Ciotti, who profiled Bukowski for

*L.A. Times Magazine,* and actor Mickey Rourke noted that although the rest of his San Pedro home was spacious and nicely appointed, Bukowski kept his writing room cramped and dingy, as if to recreate the squalid but productive environs of his past. In September 1986, Black Sparrow put out *You Get So Alone At Times That It Just Makes Sense.* This collection of poems finds Bukowski confronting his recent domesticity and ever-present thoughts of death. The lines are sparse and short, the central theme (as hinted by the title) the irremediable sadness and solitude that underlies even the most joyful of moments. Gay Brewer gives the preponderance of the word "nothing" in these poems a "two-fold" importance: "Human endeavors are illusions, not worth the life and time they demand. On the other hand, the word approaches optimism. Nothingness, which is all that exists including tedious human life, 'is worth it' (Brewer, 143).

In 1987, after eight years of hustle and frustration, Barbet Schroeder convinced a studio to fund *Barfly* at last. The two upstart Israelis behind Cannon Pictures, Menahem Golan and Yoram Globus, were as wacky and unpredictable as they were tight with their money and Schroeder was eager to start filming before they changed their minds.

Desperate for a lead with both drawing power and the talent to support the material, Schroeder offered the role of Chinaski to Mickey Rourke. Coming off the success of *9 1/2 Weeks* and entirely ignorant of Bukowski's writing, Rourke was initially hesitant to take on such an unflattering role. He came from a family of alcoholics and felt little nobility could be found in the bottom of a bottle. He also had issues with the script. Nonetheless, he was impressed by Schroeder's fire and dedication and signed on despite the low budget.

It was Rourke's idea to get Faye Dunaway to play Wanda, the Jane Cooney Baker character. Bukowski disagreed was both castings—he felt Rourke was too affected, and Dunaway too refined-looking, for their respective roles—but in the end swallowed his objections and trusted Schroeder to aptly shape their performances. Rounding out the cast was Alice Krige as Tully Sorenson, the character based on Barbara Frye. She was also much too attractive, with a long slender neck instead of Frye's deformity, but at least she was a relative unknown at the time.

Shortly after the cast was assembled, Cannon dropped a bombshell—they had no more money and the movie had to be cancelled. It was at this point that Schroeder pulled his psychotic routine, threatening to cut off a finger with a circular saw if the show did not go on as scheduled. Appreciating his commitment and flare for the dramatic, Menahem Golan found the money somewhere and gave him the go ahead.

Shooting started in February, in a real bar in Culver City, with real alcohol in the drinks, real drunks on the stools, and Bukowski on the set, getting really drunk with the extras. His initial impression of Rourke was that he was hamming it up too much, creating a caricature and not a character, but he eventually warmed up to Rourke's routine and seeing his youthful swagger portrayed so accurately released a flood of memories and engendered warm feelings toward everyone involved—well, almost everyone. In *Hollywood*, the novel he subsequently wrote about the experience of making *Barfly*, he describes Dunaway as a vain head case, more concerned with her career than getting her character right. One scene in particular—in which Chinaski and Wanda are supposed to steal green corn with the kind of desperation befitting starving drunks—struck Bukowski as artificial and flat. He was left no choice but to accept the limitations of the genre: "One doesn't expect perfection from a performance. A good imitation will do" (*Hollywood*, 171).

The film took six weeks to complete and Bukowski spent much of that time on the set, rewriting dialogue when necessary and setting Schroeder at ease whenever some minor detail went awry. By all accounts, Bukowski was accorded a surprising degree of respect by the entire cast and crew, considering how writers are more commonly treated in Hollywood. Despite his former derision of the art form, he could not help but get caught up in the thrill of it all and marveled at how far he had come from the gutter existence actually depicted in the film.

Bukowski's fame and ego received another boost in September of that year when Belgian director Dominique Deruddere released his own take on Bukowski's material. Alternately titled *Crazy Love* or *Love is a Dog from Hell*, the film faithfully captured the tone and spirit of his short fiction. Although Bukowski eventually dubbed it the best of the three films based on his work, it never received much mainstream exposure and remains difficult to track down.

*Barfly* was released to the public in December, fresh on the heels of *Crazy Love*. Many people close to its author (including Linda Lee and Marina) thought the film a total distortion of the life and individual it set out to depict, but Bukowski (perhaps out of loyalty to Schroeder) kept his gripes mostly in check. Critical reviews were lukewarm, neither condemning nor especially laudatory. Over the years, public opinion of the film has improved quite a bit and it has achieved a modest cult following, due in large part to the author's continued popularity. Regardless of its artistic merit, the movie initiated a frenzy of press on Bukowski, with magazines as disparate as Andy Warhol's *Interview* and *People* hopping on the bandwagon. Even the talk shows came calling, but after the disaster on *Apostrophe*, Bukowski knew better than to accept. Besides, his enjoyment of the limelight quickly wore off; he left early from the party following *Barfly*'s Hollywood premiere and made few public appearances thereafter.

He was in no condition for press junkets anyway. Afflicted in late December by a precipitous loss of energy, Bukowski initially chalked it up to the flu and stress brought on by the making of *Barfly* and the bustle attending its release. Blood tests revealed a general exhaustion but nothing more serious. Nevertheless, he struggled for the next nine months or so to summon the will to finish *Hollywood*, his fifth novel. He felt so poorly that he effectively stopped drinking for the first time since nearly bleeding to death in 1955. In the meantime, John Martin published *The Roominghouse Madrigals*, a large selection of early poems from 1946–1966. The lyrical and metaphorically lush pieces collected in this volume display a marked shift in style when compared to the leanness of his later poems, but Martin either decided against it or was simply unable to provide information on dates of composition and/or publishing history and that makes it difficult to trace any sort of linear progression. The overall tone is dark, with death, loneliness, and the artist as outcast providing the central themes. Perhaps Martin saw some relevance in these poems to Bukowski's tenuous state of health and advancing age. If so, his choice was rather prophetic, in light of subsequent events. In contrast, *Hollywood* is a surprisingly light-hearted *roman a clef*, given the strain of both its own birth and that of the film it chronicled. Where one might expect biting satire, fueled by the self-reproach of hard man going soft, in cahoots with an industry he despises, one finds Henry Chinaski expressing a kind of *c'est la vie* acceptance of his cushy fate, combined with a starstruck wonderment at all the insane characters he encounters. That is not to say the novel does not have its share of cynicism, social commentary, and incisive introspection—they were simply expressed more subtly than one had come to expect from Bukowski. The character of François, for example, and the practice roulette wheel that he obsessively spins in search of a winning system, seems to be a clear metaphor for Bukowski's own gambling habit, which he once admitted had put him about $10,000 in the red all told. And who can forget the scene in which a small black hand reaches through a hole in the wall of the house in the ghetto where Jon and François are living, groping for something, anything to steal. The stark poverty that exists in the midst of Hollywood's extravagant wealth has seldom been more vividly evoked.

The effort to complete *Hollywood* was so draining that the morning following its completion found Bukowski wracked with a high fever, unable to eat or sleep. The crisis lasted a week, only to be followed by two more such attacks of nearly equal length. Visits to high-priced doctors in Beverly Hills returned no diagnosis besides anemia, which hardly accounted for the fevers or his loss in appetite. His weight plummeted, from over 200 lbs to a mere 168; his hairline receded; and his face grew sallow and skeletal. Lying in bed, the words of "Old Man, Dead in a Room," first published so long ago in issue number one of *The Outsider* and newly resurrected for *The Roominghouse Madrigals*, must have come back to him with striking poignancy:

it's not death
but dying will solve its power
and as my grey hands
drop a last desperate pen
in some cheap room
they will find me there
and never know
my name
my meaning
nor the treasure
of my escape

(*Roominghouse Madrigals,* 54)

In the end, it was Bukowski's lifelong love of cats, of all things, that probably saved his life. Ever since moving into his place in San Pedro, his habit of taking in strays had led to more and more feline friends, to the point where Bukowski began proselytizing the physical and psychological benefits of the practice (fellow writer William Burroughs, another longtime survivor of excessive self-abuse, held the same beliefs). A series of extemporaneous remarks to Sean Penn, compiled in 1987 for a feature in *Interview* magazine (and later included in *Drinking with Bukowski*) contained the following thoughts on cats:

Having a bunch of cats around is good. If you're feeling bad, you just look at the cats, you'll feel better, because they know that everything is, just as it is. There's nothing to get excited about. They just know. They're saviors. The more cats you have, the longer you live. If you have a hundred cats, you'll live ten times longer than if you have ten. Someday this will be discovered, and people will have a thousand cats and live forever. It's truly ridiculous.

(Weizman, ed., 188)

Maybe so, but no more ridiculous than a veterinarian diagnosing an illness that had stymied the best physicians in Los Angeles. While accompanying one of his familiars on a routine check-up, Bukowski started talking with the vet about his symptoms and the vet suggested he get tested for tuberculosis, an affliction not unheard of in felines but a real rarity in late 20th-century humans, especially those living the good life in Southern California.

Sure enough, the tests came back positive. Howard Sounes theorizes that Bukowski was infected as a toddler by his Uncle John, who died of consumption, and that the disease lay dormant until his late-life exhaustion allowed it to gain a foothold on his immune system, but it is every bit as likely that he contracted it in one of the rat-infested flophouses he patronized in the '40s and '50s. Whatever the case, one positive result of the whole ordeal was that Bukowski's inadvertent sobriety was strictly enforced during a six-month course of strong antibiotics and he never regained his taste for immoderate drinking. That long overdue lifestyle change boosted his longevity as much as any proximate herd of cats.

Bukowski celebrated his 70th birthday in 1990 with the release of *Septuagenarian Stew*, a 400-page assemblage of 20 stories and about twice that many poems. Feeling long in the tooth evidently convinced him to give his work wider reign, resulting in lengthier works in both formats. Many of the stories also feature characters in significantly better financial situations than those in past collections, betraying a keen awareness of his own change in fortune, but, tellingly, their solvent bank accounts do not exempt them from the same sort of crises and misfortunes that befell their skid row antecedents (Brewer, 76). One notable exception to Bukowski's new cast of middle-class protagonists is the titular character in the rightfully lauded story "The Life of a Bum," which retains Bukowski's diehard animosity towards all those who mindlessly uphold the status quo, a stance that gained new relevance with readers in the fallout from the money-centric '80s.

The poems in *Septuagenarian Stew* continue the explorations of death and aging begun in earlier collections (most notably *You Get So Alone At Times That It Just Makes Sense*), but carry the stamp of a man coming to grips with the inevitable and a clear-eyed gratitude for having lived that long. The question of his literary legacy also looms large; names of his forbears litter the page as if their invocation might lend him some of their staying power.

Recognizing the growing limitations of his aging eyes (Bukowski eventually had surgery to remove cataracts in 1992) and slipping dexterity, but leery of upsetting a long-entrenched method of creation, Linda Lee toyed with the idea of buying Bukowski a computer. After consulting Marina (who was then a newly out-of-work aerospace engineer) and divining his opinion on the matter without ruining the surprise, she decided on an Apple IIsi and gave it to him for Christmas in 1990 (Sounes, 221). Though he joked about losing his mojo, and struggled through a requisite period of adjustment, his newfangled typer turned out to be a godsend. A letter to Jon Cone, editor of *World Letter,* has Bukowski sounding like an early computer advertisement, complete with promises of lifestyle improvement:

> Once you get in to these things you'll hate a typewriter if you ever have to go back to it, such things as ribbons, carbons, white-outs and hand shifting, etc. will seem stupid and galling. You correct your copy right off the screen. The computer even corrects your spelling for you. And you can save all your work on disks which can be filed into a small space, any portion of which can be reprinted in as many copies as you wish. And the copy just looks so much better than typewritten copy. Everything saves you hours and those hours can be used as you wish[:] sleep, drink, go to movie, pet your cat, walk your dog, take a bath, muse. For me, actually, it has doubled my creative output and somehow strengthened it.
>
> (*Reach for the Sun,* 274)

The result of this boost in productivity was of avalanche of new material and the release, in 1992, of his largest book of poetry to date. *The Last Night of the Earth Poems* is over 400 pages long and picks up right where *Septuagenarian Stew* left off, assessing the state of his art, body, and soul and looking ahead to the end of it all. There is also a preoccupation with illness hovering over the collection, to such an extant that one might be tempted to interpret it as a presentiment of what came next.

One influence on Bukowski's writing seldom mentioned, by him or anyone else, before the publication of *Pulp,* is the so-called "hardboiled" prose of mystery writers like Raymond Chandler, Dashiell Hammett, and, later, James Ellroy. In all likelihood, this was because they too still lacked the critical recognition they deserved and were inextricably localized by the Southern California settings they most often chose for their dark tales of dastardly intrigue and treacherous dames. Nowadays, getting caught reading *The Big Sleep* or *The Maltese Falcon* on a bus or beach is a badge of hip sophistication but in Bukowski's time such material was deemed sordid, and slightly perverted. Bukowski was not consciously following any trends when he decided to make his sixth novel a paean to the genre, but he was insuring his own affinity with its early progenitors would not go unnoticed. Work on *Pulp* began in 1991 but Bukowski struggled mightily with the plotting requirements (See *Reach for the Sun*, pp. 237, 245, 262, and 271) and then got bogged down by something much much worse.

This time the doctors had no problem reaching a diagnosis. Bukowski was suffering from myelogenous leukemia, a form of cancer that attacks the white blood cells in bone marrow and eventually spreads to other parts of the body. The prognosis was even worse—without treatment he could only expect to live another six months.

Ever the fighter, Bukowski consented to undergoing chemotherapy. He checked into San Pedro Peninsula Hospital in early spring 1993, and stayed there for seven weeks. The treatments were grueling; in another letter to Jon Cone, he wrote: "They just about blast the shit out of you, killing most of the blood cells and plenty of other parts" (*Reach for the Sun*, 287). Rumors began to fly that Bukowski was already dead, some of which reached the ears of friends who did not know any different (Sounes, 236). A letter to William Packard proved the rumors were not far wrong: "A few nights of horror. Almost kicked it twice," Bukowski reports, laconic and unadorned to the end (*Reach for the Sun*, 288).

The chemotherapy treatments successfully sent the cancer into remission but Bukowski was realistic about his prospects. "Yes, I know about hospitals and death-bed bits, seems like I've come close so many times. I'm going to make it one of these tries: practice makes perfect" (*Reach for the Sun*, 291).

Fearful of leaving *Pulp* unfinished, he knocked off his schlocky hero Nick Belane with a hail of gunfire. Vesting himself against the near certainty of getting similarly gut-shot by both critics and fans of his previous work, he dedicated the book to "bad writing" and told everyone who asked that it was certain to ruin his reputation, though not without the mischievous glee of a lifelong provocateur. His real disappointment came from reading *Hank, The Life of Charles Bukowski*, the biography of him his old friend and disciple Neeli Cherkovski had published in 1991. "It is virtually unreadable. Very bad writing. Dull, inept. I gave Neeli hours of tape, really good stuff, of wild and wonderful times, crazy times, deadly times but he put *none* of it in" (*Reach for the Sun*, 281). Worse than producing an unsatisfying biography—in all fairness, Bukowski was constitutionally indisposed to the format and though *Hank* (later revised and reprinted as *Bukowski: A Life*) contains a number of factual errors, it is hardly as bad as Bukowski claims and in all likelihood he would have had harsh words for anyone who dared to tell his story, present company included—was Cherkovski's apparent carelessness with some original photos and "other materials" that were subsequently lost forever (*Reach for the Sun*, 282).

Aiding his recovery from the disappointment attending *Hank* was an unexpected visit from Carl Weissner, as well as Black Sparrow's publication of his first volume of correspondence (*Screams from the Balcony: Selected Letters 1960–1970*) and the 1993 release of *Run with the Hunted*, a 500-page retrospective collection from HarperCollins. This excellent "Bukowski Reader" culls some of his best prose and poetry from dozens of different publications and arranges them chronologically. Both books brought back fond memories of those heady days when he was just starting out and, in effect let Bukowski retell his own life story. An extra ego kick and legacy assurance came when William Packard, a close friend and editor of the *New York Quarterly*, sent word that he was teaching from *Run with the Hunted* in his class at N.Y.U. Perhaps academic acceptance was not out of the question after all.

By this time, Bukowski could also be certain that Linda would be well taken care of after his death. Sales of his books were stronger than ever; monthly royalties from Black Sparrow alone had swelled to $7,000, "an unbelievable sum" compared to the $100 per month he was paid in 1970 (*Reach for the Sun*, 273).

Towards the end, hoping to help fill the aimless hours with meaningful activity (he was often too weak to write) and eager to try alternative remedies, Linda Lee convinced Bukowski to take up transcendental meditation and ayurvedic healing. It is hard to think of a more incongruous image than the author of "the proud thin dying" ("among other lies, / they were taught that silence was / bravery," *Run with the Hunted*, 399) sitting Indian-style, facing his demise with stillness and inner harmony, but Bukowski saw it as just another way of fighting back: "Who the hell knows? Some direction, some pathway, instead of sitting around waiting" (*Reach for the Sun*, 297).

Nonetheless, the cancer resurfaced in the fall of 1993, and rather than trying to further postpone the inevitable with tortuous chemo treatments, Bukowski decided he would rather spend his last days at home. Unfortunately a bout of pneumonia forced a return to the hospital, where Bukowski beat back the virus but ultimately succumbed to the leukemia a week after he was admitted. The unsung laureate of San Pedro died March 9, 1994, at the age of 73.

Like his wedding to Linda Lee, Bukowski's funeral was a fairly private affair, held at the chapel in Green Hills Memorial Park, the cemetery overlooking San Pedro Bay where Bukowski was buried. In attendance were Linda, Marina, Gerald Locklin (who provides an account of the services and interment in *Drinking with Bukowski*), Sholom "Red" Stodolsky (friend and owner of Baroque Books in Hollywood), John Thomas, Philomene Long, Carl Weissner, Sean Penn, John Martin, and several other neighbors and friends. Weissner, Penn, and Martin gave brief eulogies. Buddhist monks conducted the services—an odd coda to the bawdy barroom ballad that represented the majority of his life, perhaps, but not entirely inconsistent with his mindset when last call was announced, especially in light of his chosen epitaph. Above the simple icon of a boxer and the dates of his life are two simple words: "Don't try." Although many have interpreted this as some kind of nihilist credo, his real meaning has more to do with his anti-intellectual approach to writing and to life, as strongly supported by two corollary quotes. The first, which comes from a December 28, 1980 letter to fan Joe Stapen, reads "Somebody once asked me what my theory of life was and I said, 'Don't try.' That fits the writing too. I don't try, I just type, and if I say any more than that, I'm trying" (*Reach for the Sun*, 21). The second, and more commonly bandied about of the two, unfortunately lacks a source:

> Somebody at one of these places asked me: 'What do you do? How do you write, create?' You don't, I told them. You don't try. That's very important: not to try, either for Cadillacs, creation or immortality. You wait, and if nothing happens, you wait some more. It's like a bug high on the wall. You wait for it to come to you. When it gets close enough you reach out, slap out and kill it. Or if you like it's looks, you make a pet out of it.

Most of the American obituaries perpetuated the popular myth of Bukowski by focusing only on the sordid aspects of his life and giving short shrift to a massive and varied body of work that would only continue to grow in size as John Martin kept the faith with a steady stream of posthumous releases. Abetting this unfortunate transformation of the living, breathing man and writer into a monolithic caricature and involuntary cult figurehead are the legion of his fans that think they honor him by genuflecting at his grave and proclaiming his greatness with bull-horn insistence. A small excerpt of just one sample will go a long way towards explaining what I mean. Though written while Bukowski was still alive, David Barker's *The King of San Pedro* (Richard G. Wong & Co., 1985) provides perhaps the best example; given the tiny size of this miniature book (2 1/8" x 2 5/8"), the strident prose inside grows all the more ridiculous:

> It's nearly 2,000 years since Christ hung on a cross and 90 minutes to Armageddon, and the pyramids are crumbling while Charles

Bukowski looks out over San Pedro Bay through eyes like those of some reptilian beast, some cold-blooded heir to the earth. That's where I place Bukowski, poised between the murder of Christ and the last battle over men's souls. Jeering the angels, but no friend of the devil either. Merely waiting for the end with god-like patience and indifference, a drunken Buddha of negativity, the supremely frozen man.

(Barker, 9–10)

This speaks for itself. It is hardly necessary to speculate on what Bukowski thought about such hagiography. The ugly fact of the matter is Bukowski once spit in Barker's face in the 49er Tavern after a reading at Long Beach State and then Barker proudly published an account of the experience (included in *Drinking with Bukowski*).

Some may counter that Bukowski did the exact same thing during his lifetime, intentionally building the myth poem by poem, story by story, article by article until even he believed it. But anyone who reads his work closely will see the irony in it, the tongue-in-check self-deprecation and the crushing self-doubt. Towards the end of his life Bukowski was asked to appear on everything from Johnny Carson to *60 Minutes* (*Reaching for the Sun*, 97). He turned them all down, not because he was trying to maintain an isolationist, anti-establishment image, but because he had simply grown tired of talking about himself (*Reaching for the Sun*, 65).

People that knew Bukowski best are quick to deconstruct the myth and set the story straight. After reading his own words (particularly the letters), their testimonies are the ones to turn to when searching for the truth. Bukowski's close friend and late night confidante John Thomas probably said it best in an essay written years earlier but resurrected for inclusion in his own quirky tribute, *Bukowski in the Bathtub*:

Hank's image and his reputation are largely moonshine (I intend no pun), which makes him the rarest type of celebrity this silly town could spawn. He is sane, he is normal, he is neither beautiful nor arrestingly ugly, he draws his strength from solitude, and his best work is solid and thoughtful. ( ... )

... Please, Los Angeles, consider the unlikely nature of your good fortune and don't waste Charles Bukowski! Make no more corny Bukowski myths, and simply let the old one die.

(Long, ed., 86–87)

Barker, David. *The King of San Pedro*. Del Mar, CA: Richard G. Wong & Co., 1985.

Brewer, Gay. *Charles Bukowski*. New York: Twayne Publishers, 1997.

Bukowski, Charles. *Notes of a Dirty Old Man*. San Francisco: City Lights Books, 1973.

————. *Love Poem to Marina*. Santa Rosa: Black Sparrow, 1973.

————. *Ham on Rye*. Santa Rosa: Black Sparrow Press, 1982.

————. *Hollywood*. San Rosa: Black Sparrow Press, 1989.

————. *Screams from the Balcony: Selected Letters 1960–1970 (Volume 1)*, ed. Seamus Cooney. Santa Rosa: Black Sparrow Press, 1993.

————. *Living on Luck: Selected Letters 1960s–1970s 9 (Volume 2)*, ed. Seamus Cooney. Santa Rosa: Black Sparrow Press, 1995.

————. *Reach for the Sun: Selected Letters 1978–1994 (Volume 3)*, ed. Seamus Cooney. Santa Rosa: Black Sparrow Press, 1999.

Cherkovski, Neeli. *Bukowski: A Life*. South Royalton: Steerforth Press, 1999.

Christy, Jim & Powell, Claude. *The Buk Book: Musings on Charles Bukowski*. Toronto: ECW Press, 1997.

Cooney, Seamus, ed. *The Bukowski/Purdy Letters: A Decade of Dialogue, 1964–1974*. Santa Barbara: Paget Press, 1983.

Harrison, Russell. *Against the American Dream: Essays on Charles Bukowski*. Santa Rosa: Black Sparrow Press, 1994.

Krumhansl, Aaron. *A Descriptive Bibliography of the Primary Publications of Charles Bukowski*. Santa Rosa: Black Sparrow Press, 1999.

Long, Philomene, ed. *Bukowski in the Bathtub: Recollections of Charles Bukowski by John Thomas*. Venice, CA: Raven/Temple of Man, 1997.

Moore, Steven, ed. *Beerspit and Night Cursing: The Correspondence of Charles Bukowski and Sheri Martinelli 1960–1967*. Santa Rosa: Black Sparrow Press, 2001.

Smith, Joan Jobe. *Das ist Alles: Charles Bukowski Recollected.* Long Beach: Pearl Editions, 1995.

Sounes, Howard. *Charles Bukowski: Locked in the Arms of a Crazy Life.* New York: Grove, 1998

Weizman, Daniel, ed. *Drinking with Bukowski: Recollections of the Poet Laureate of Skid Row.* New York: Thunder's Mouth Press, 2000

1920 Heinrich Karl is born August 16 in Andernach, Germany to Henry Charles Bukowski, an American soldier, and Katharina Fett, a German seamstress.

1923 Henry Sr. moves his wife and son to the United States, settling initially in Baltimore and then returning to California.

1924–27 Family moves several times around Los Angeles, settling at 2122 Longwood Ave; beatings begin when Bukowski fails to meet his father's exacting standards for mowing the lawn.

1931–32 Bukowski's fifth-grade teacher singles out his essay submission on President Hoover's visit for special praise; however, the essay is a complete fabrication; starts to take refuge in public libraries, reading Hemingway, Lawrence, and Dos Passos.

1934–39 Attends Los Angles High School; develops acute case of *acne vulgaris* and withdraws from his peers; misses a semester while undergoing treatment; writes first short story.

1939–41 Gets and loses job at Sears & Roebuck; attends L.A. City College on scholarship; stirs up controversy by supporting Hitler; returns home one day to find his stories and clothes thrown out on the lawn by his father; moves out, finds lodging downtown.

1941–42 Drops out of college; takes a bus to New Orleans, inaugurating a period of itinerancy; takes odd jobs all over the country, seldom lasting more than a week; writes and submits stories to several major publications.

1944 "Aftermath of a Lengthy Rejection Slip" accepted by *Story*; arrested in Philadelphia for alleged draft dodging; spends 17 days in Moyamensing Prison before a psychiatrist releases him as unfit for military service.

1946 Returns to Los Angeles; "20 Tanks from Kasseldown" published in *Portfolio* alongside Genet, Sartre, Lorca, and

Miller; pens and publishes a few poems but otherwise quits writing during a decade-long drinking binge.

1947–51　Returns to L.A. again and lives with parents before finding his own place; meets Jane Cooney Baker; multiple arrests for public drunkenness; takes a temporary job at the post office during the Christmas rush.

1952　Signs on with the post office full-time for a three-year stint.

1955　Nearly dies from a massive hemorrhage; diagnosed with a bleeding ulcer and told by doctors to quit drinking; Jane introduces him to betting at the horsetrack; submits poems to *Harlequin* and editor Barbara Frye shows interest in more than his poetry—he jokingly proposes to her in a letter; marries Frye in Las Vegas October 29, 1955.

1956　Bukowski's mother, Katherine, dies of cancer; he returns to his job at the post office.

1958　Frye and Bukowski grow apart and are divorced on March 18; Henry, Sr. dies in December of a heart attack; Bukowski inherits house and $15,000–16,000, some of which he blows on drink and at the racetrack.

1959–61　Numerous poems appear in the small press; first chapbook, *Flower, Fist and Bestial Wail,* published by Hearse Press; begins corresponding with dozens of editors, publishers, and fellow writers; reconnects with Jane Cooney Baker.

1962　Jane Cooney Baker dies of excessive drinking on January 22; Bukowski meets and begins relationship with Frances Smith (a.k.a. FrancEyE); two more chapbooks published, *Longshot Pomes for Broke Players* and *Run with the Hunted.*

1963　Voted "Outsider of the Year" by *The Outsider* magazine (volume 3 features many of his poems); editors/publishers Jon and "Gypsy Lou" Webb give him a Loujon

Press award and handprint *It Catches My Heart in Its Hands: New and Selected Poems 1955–1963*; FrancEyE gets pregnant and moves in with Bukowski at De Longpre Ave.

1964    The Webbs pay a visit, firm up plans for a second poetry collection; Marina Louise Bukowski is born September 7; tensions mount between Bukowski and FrancEyE.

1965    Trip to New Orleans in March; while there, writes bulk of the poems that appear in *Crucifix in a Deathhand*, published a month later by Loujon Press in a lavish edition; *Cold Dogs in the Courtyard and Confessions of a Man Insane Enough to Live with Beasts* also published; meets John Martin; FrancEyE moves out with Marina, partially supported by Bukowski.

1966    Maintains correspondence with many editors and publishers in the small press; receives letter from Carl Weissner, a German fan who would become his translator and agent abroad; John Martin founds Black Sparrow Press and publishes a handful of Bukowski broadsides.

1967    Begins writing "Notes of a Dirty Old Man" column for *Open City*, a Los Angeles underground newspaper; more Black Sparrow broadsides.

1968    Local fame grows; *At Terror Street and Agony Way* published in May by Black Sparrow; another small press puts out *Poems Written before Jumping Out of an 8 Story Window* later that summer; Post Office officials investigate his "obscene" writing for *Open City*.

1969    Founds his own magazine, *Laugh Literary and Man the Humping Guns*, with disciple Neeli Cherkovski (three issues, '69–72); published alongside Harold Norse and Philip Lamantia in Penguin Modern Poets Series, no. 13; Essex house publishes *Notes of a Dirty Old Man* collection; *The Days Run Away Like Wild Horses over the Hills* is released by Black Sparrow; after fifteen years on the job, resigns from post office to avoid being fired and convinces John Martin to provide a $100-per-month stipend; gives first public reading at The Bridge.

1970   Finishes *Post Office*, his first novel, in 21 days; sells personal papers to UC Santa Barbara; gives more readings; meets Linda King.

1971   *Post Office* is published; Jon Webb dies, estranged from Bukowski over the latter's depictions of him in *Open City*; tumultuous affair with Linda King.

1972   Co-edits *Anthology of L.A. Poets*; Ferlinghetti's City Lights publishes first story collection, *Erections, Ejaculations, Exhibitions and General Tales of Ordinary Madness*; Black Sparrow prints *Mockingbird Wish Me Luck*; affair with Liza Williams.

1973   Taylor Hackford documentary, *Bukowski*, shown on LA public television, wins "best cultural program" awar.d; *South of No North* is published; moves in with King in Silver Lake; Carl Weissner translates some of *Erections ...* into German; Bukowski wins $5000 grant from the NEA.

1974   *Poems Written before Jumping out of an 8 Story Window* (German translations, not the same as earlier book) sells 50,000 copies in Germany, other publications sell even better; *Burning in Water Drowning in Flame: Selected Poems 1955–1973*; raises reading fee to $1,000.

1975–77   Affair with Linda King ends after she has a miscarriage; Bukowski chases Pamela Miller, a.k.a. Cupcakes; has dozens of brief affairs and one-night stands; *Factotum*, his second novel, is published; meets Linda Lee Beighle and settles down; *Love is a Dog from Hell* is published.

1978   Barbet Schroeder contacts him about a possible film project; travels to Germany with Linda Lee for book promotion and reading in Hamburg, visits with Carl Weissner, and his Uncle Heinrich in Andernach birthplace; returns to Europe in May for infamous appearance on French talk

124

show, *Apostrophe*; third novel, *Women*, is published in December; buys a house in San Pedro (and a BMW, in '79) to defray taxes on booming royalties.

1979   Begins work on screenplay for *Barfly*; *Play the Piano Drunk like a Percussion Instrument Until the Fingers Begin to Bleed a Bit* is published; travelogue of trip to Germany, *Shakespeare Never Did This*, published with photos by Michael Montfort.

1980–87   *Barfly* is stuck in financing limbo; Schroeder makes documentary, *The Charles Bukowski Tapes*; string of books are published by Black Sparrow: *Dangling in the Tournefortia* (1981), *Ham on Rye* (1982), *Hot Water Music* (1983), and *War All the Time* (1984); marries Linda Lee August 18, 1985; other films based on his works: *Tales of Ordinary Madness*, 1983 (U.S. release) and *Crazy Love* (a.k.a. *Love* is a *Dog from Hell*), 1987.

1987   Filming begins on *Barfly*; premieres in December, starring Mickey Rourke and Faye Dunaway.

1988–1993   Falls ill with tuberculosis, barely recovers; *The Roominghouse Madrigals: Early Selected Poems 1946–1966* (1988), *Hollywood* (1989), *Septuagenarian Stew* (1990), *The Last Night on Earth Poems* (1992), *Screams from the Balcony: Selected Letters 1960–1970* (1993), and *Run with the Hunter: A Charles Bukowski Reader* are published (1993).

1993   Diagnosed with leukemia; undergoes chemotherapy treatment; cancer returns in the fall of 1993, then pneumonia and infection; at Linda Lee's prompting, becomes interested in Buddhism.

1994   Bukowski dies of leukemia March 9; funeral is held on March 14, with ceremony performed by Buddhist monks; many posthumous publications follow.

*Flower, Fist and Bestial Wall* (1960)

*Longshot Poems for Broke Players* (1962)

*Run with the Hunted* (1962)

*It Catches My Heart in Its Hand* (1963)

*Crucifix in a Deathhand* (1965)

*Cold Dogs in the Courtyard* (1965)

*Confessions of a Man Insane Enough to Live with Beasts* (1965)

*All the Assholes in the World and Mine* (1966)

*The Curtains Are Waving ...* (1967)

*Poems Written Before Jumping out of an 8 Story Window* (1968)

*At Terror Street and Agony Way* (1968)

*A Bukowski Sampler*, ed. Douglas Blazek (1969)

*Notes of a Dirty Old Man* (1969)

*Days Run Away Like Wild Horses Over the Hills* (1969)

*Fire Station* (1970)

*Another Academy* (1970)

*Post Office* (1971)

*Anthology of L.A. Poets*, eds. Bukowski, Neeli Cherry, and Paul Vangelisti (1972)

*Mockingbird, Wish Me Luck* (1972)

*Erections, Ejaculations, Exhibitions and General Tales of Ordinary Madness*, ed. Gail Chiarello (1972)

*South of No North* (1973)

*Burning in Water Drowning in Flame: Selected Poems 1955–1973* (1974)

*Factotum* (1975)

*Scarlet* (1976)

*Love is a Dog from Hell* (1977)

*Women* (1978)

*You Kissed Lilly* (1978)

*Play the Piano Drunk Like a Percussion Instrument Until the Fingers Begin to Bleed a Bit* (1979)

*Shakespeare Never Did This* (1979)

*Dangling in the Tournefortia* (1981)

*Ham on Rye* (1982)

*Hot Water Music* (1983)

*Bring Me Your Love* (1983)

*There's No Business* (1984)

*War All the Time: Poems 1981–1984* (1984)

*You Get So Alone at Times It Just Makes Sense* (1986)

*The Movie Barfly* (1987)

*A Visitor Complains of My Disenfanchise* (1987)

*Roominghouse Madrigals: Early Selected Poems 1946–1966* (1988)

*Hollywood* (1989)

*Septuagenarian Stew: Stories and Poems* (1990)

*People Poems* (1991)

*Bluebird* (1991)

*In the Shadow of the Rose* (1991)

*Three Poems* (1992)

*Last Night of the Earth Poems* (1992)

*Run with the Hunted: A Charles Bukowski Reader*, ed. John Martin (1993)

*Screams from the Balcony: Selected Letters 1960–1970, Volume 1*, ed. Seamus Cooney (1993)

*Pulp* (1994)

*Shakespeare Never Did This* (Augmented Edition) (1995)

*Living on Luck: Selected Letters 1960s–1970s, Volume 2*, ed. Seamus Cooney (1995)

*Betting on the Muse: Poems & Stories* (1996)

*Bone Palace Ballet: New Poems* (1997)

*The Captain Is Out to Lunch and the Sailors Have Taken over the Ship* (Ill. R. Crumb) (1998)

*What Matters Most Is How Well You Walk Through the Fire* (1999)

*Reach For The Sun: Selected Letters 1978–1994, Volume 3*, ed. Seamus Cooney (1999)

*Open All Night: New Poems* (2000)

*The Night Torn Mad with Footsteps* (2001)

*The Flash of Lightning Behind the Mountain: New Poems* (2004)

## ■ BIBLIOGRAPHY

Cherkovski, Neeli. *Whitman's Wild Children*. Venice, CA: Lapis Press, 1988.

Christy, Ana and Dave, eds. *Charles Bukowski and Alpha Beat Press, 1988–1994*. New Hope, PA: Alpha Beat Press, 1994.

Ciotti, Paul. "Bukowski." *Los Angeles Times Magazine*, March 22, 1987.

Dorbin, Sanford M. *A Bibliography of Charles Bukowski*. Los Angeles: Black Sparrow Press, 1969.

Dougherty, Jay. "Charles Bukowski and the Outlaw Spirit." *Gargoyle* 35 (1988): 92–103

Duval, Jean-François. *Bukowski and the Beats*. Northville, Michigan: Sun Dog Press, 2002.

Esterly, Glenn. "Buk: The Pock-Marked Poetry of Charles Bukowski." *Rolling Stone*, June 17, 1976: 28–34.

Fogel, Al. *Charles Bukowski: A Comprehensive Checklist*. Miami: Sole Proprietor Press, 1982.

Fox, Hugh. *Charles Bukowski: A Critical and Bibliographical Study*. Somerville, Mass.: Abyss Publications, 1971.

Glover, David. "A Day at the Races: Gambling and Luck in Bukowski's Fiction." *Review of Contemporary Fiction* 5.3 (Fall 1985): 32–33.

Harrison, Russell. "The Letters of Charles Bukowski." *Sure, the Charles Bukowski Newsletter* 8–9 (1993): 17–29.

Joyce, William. *Miller, Bukowski, and Their Enemies: Essays on Contemporary Culture*. Greensboro, N.C.: Avisson Press, 1996

Locklin, Gerald. *Charles Bukowski: A Sure Bet*. Sudbury, Mass.: Water Row Press, 1996.

Malone, Aubrey. *The Hunchback of East Hollywood: A Biography of Charles Bukowski*. Manchester: Critical Vision, 2003.

Pivano, Fernanda. *Charles Bukowski: Laughing with the Gods*. Northville, Michigan: Sun Dog Press, 2000.

Richmond, Steve. *Spinning off Bukowski*. Northville, Michigan: Sun Dog Press, 1996.

Sherman, Jory. *Bukowski: Friendship, Fame & Bestial Myth*. Augusta, GA: Blue Horse Publications, 1981.

Smith, Joan Jobe, ed. *Das ist Alles: Bukowski in Recollection*. Long Beach, CA: Pearl Editions, 1995.

Sounes, Howard. *Bukowski in Pictures*. Edinburgh: Rebel Inc., 2000.

Wennersten, Robert. "Paying for Horses: An Interview with Charles Bukowski." *London Magazine*. December 1974–January 1975, 35–54.

Winans, A.D. *The Charles Bukowski/Second Coming Years*. Warwickshire, England: Beat Scene Press, 1996.

———. *Remembering Bukowski*. San Pedro, CA: Lummox Press, 1999.

———. *The Holy Grail: Charles Bukowski and the Second Coming Revolution*. Paradise, CA: Dustbooks, 2002.

**WEBSITES**

**The Academy of American Poets—Charles Bukowski**
http://www.poets.org/poets/poets.cfm

**Anti-Hero Art**
http://www.anti-heroart.com/buk.html

**Charles Bukowski**
http://www.levity.com/corduroy/bukowski.htm

**Charles Bukowski: These Words I Write Keep Me from Total Madness**
http://www.levee67.com/bukowski/introduction.html

**Charles Bukowski**
http://www.beatmuseum.org/bukowski/bukmain.html

**Charles Bukowski Timeline**
http://www.uwec.edu/lyonsaj/authorsinfo/bukowskibio.htm

MICHAEL GRAY BAUGHAN is a freelance writer living in the San Francisco Bay Area. He is the contributing editor of volumes on E.E. Cummings and John Ashbery in Harold Bloom's Major Poets series (Chelsea House), and another on Rudyard Kipling in the Short Story Writer's series. As a compositor and/or production editor, he has also recently worked on a number of music-related titles from Backbeat Books, including *American Basses* (2002), *45 RPM* (1999), *The Hammond Organ* (2002, 2nd ed.) and *Playing from the Heart* (2002). Michael and his wife Lizzie are the proud parents of twin girls, Ella and Callie.

GAYLORD BREWER is a poet and critic who teaches in the English Department at Middle Tennessee State University and edits the journal *Poems and Plays*. He is the author of *Charles Bukowski* (1997) in the Twayne Author Series, as well as numerous other publications. His book of poetry, *Devilfish* (1999), has recently won the Red Hen Poetry Prize. His most recent books of poetry are *Barbaric Mercies* (2003) and *Exit Pursued by a Bear* (2004).